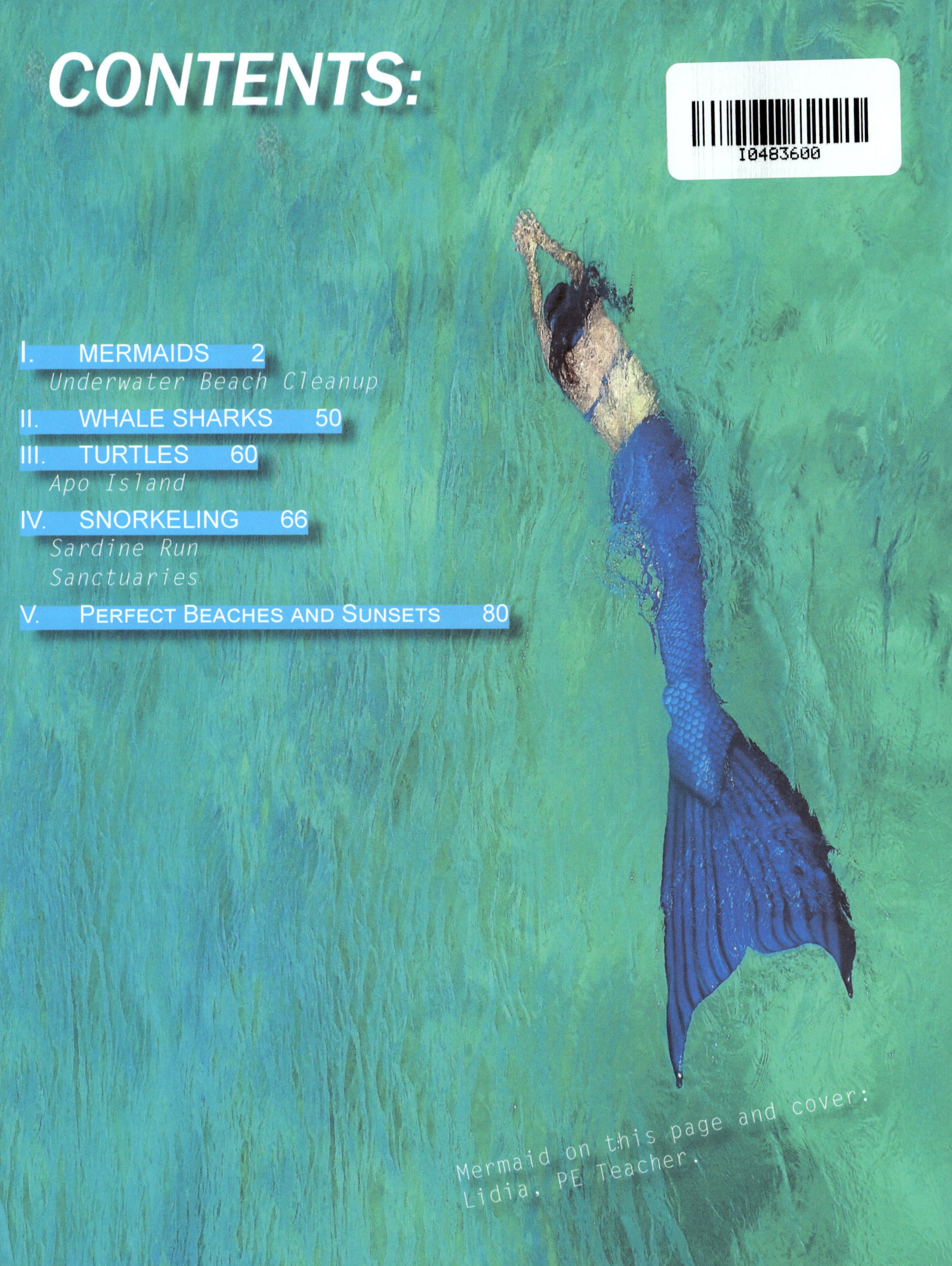

CONTENTS:

Mermaid on this page and cover:
Lidia, PE Teacher.

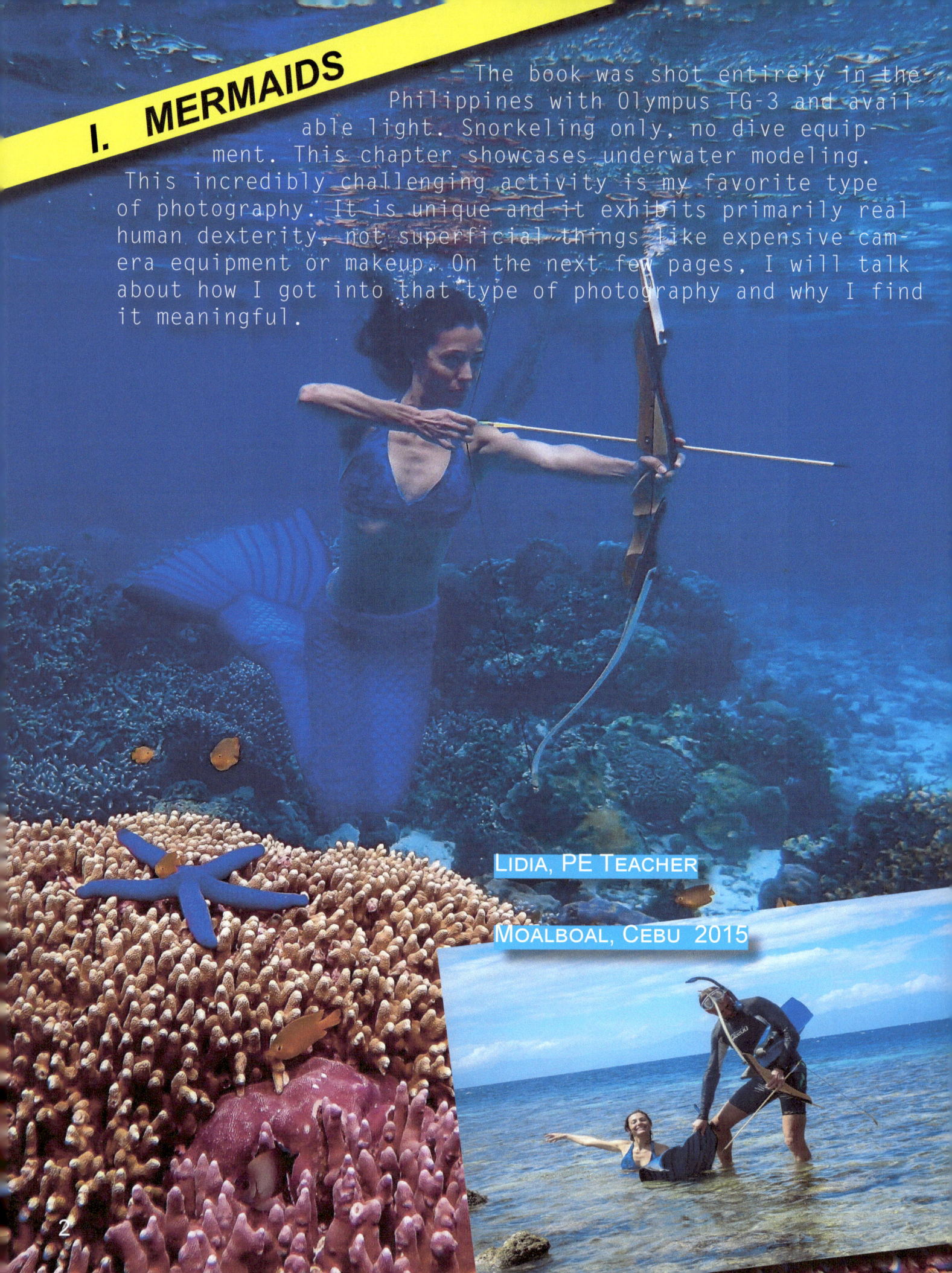

The book was shot entirely in the Philippines with Olympus TG-3 and available light. Snorkeling only, no dive equipment. This chapter showcases underwater modeling. This incredibly challenging activity is my favorite type of photography. It is unique and it exhibits primarily real human dexterity, not superficial things like expensive camera equipment or makeup. On the next few pages, I will talk about how I got into that type of photography and why I find it meaningful.

LIDIA, PE TEACHER

MOALBOAL, CEBU 2015

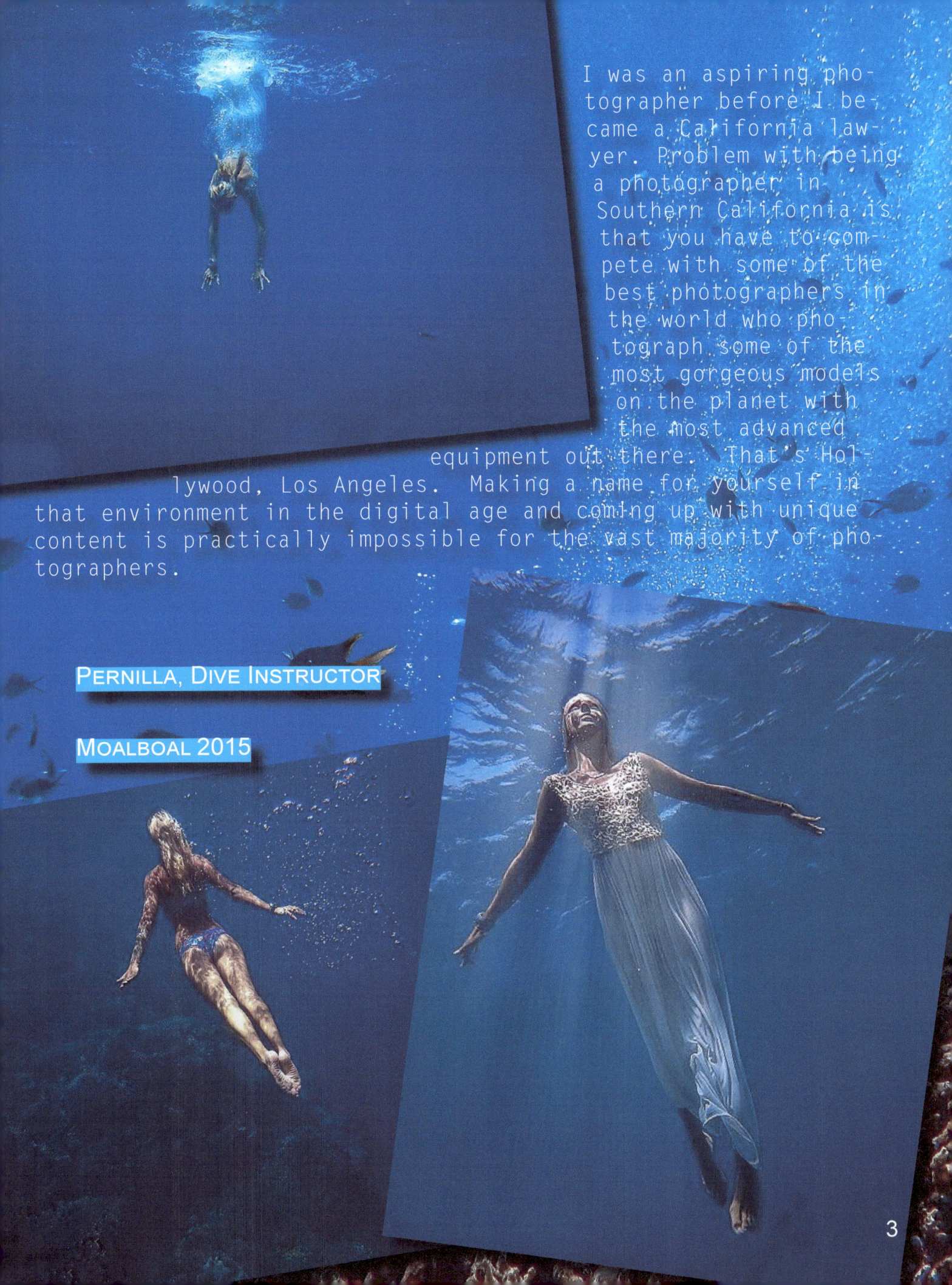

I was an aspiring photographer before I became a California lawyer. Problem with being a photographer in Southern California is that you have to compete with some of the best photographers in the world who photograph some of the most gorgeous models on the planet with the most advanced equipment out there. That's Hollywood, Los Angeles. Making a name for yourself in that environment in the digital age and coming up with unique content is practically impossible for the vast majority of photographers.

PERNILLA, DIVE INSTRUCTOR

MOALBOAL 2015

3

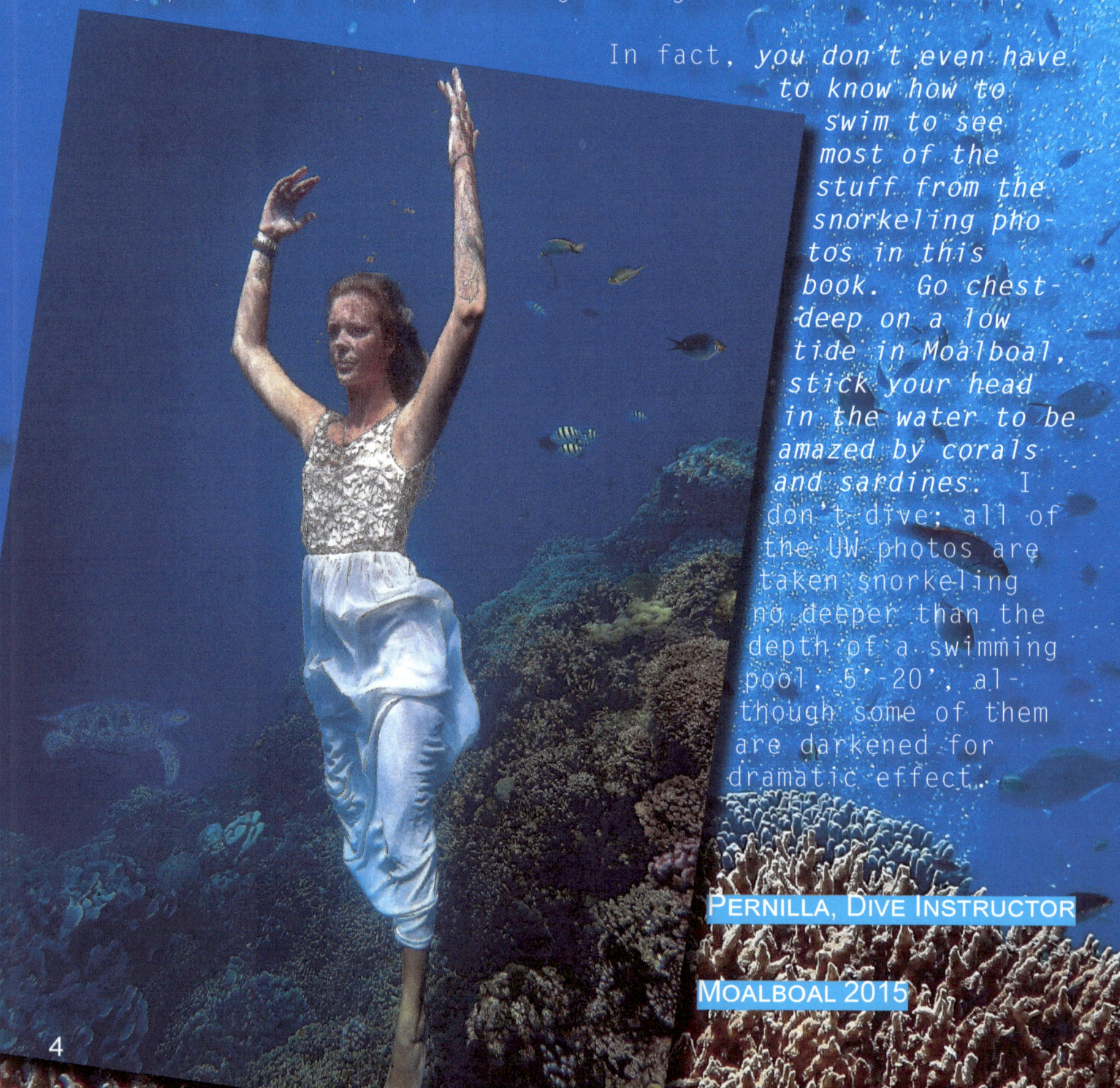

Fortunately for me, even the best photographers in America do not have easy everyday access to some of the best underwater scenery (free backdrops) in the world. This is where I saw an opportunity to make my mark in photography by trying to contribute something unique and fresh to this art form. In the Philippines, you don't need expensive equipment to take mind-blowing photos. *All you need is to be there.* Chances are, there will be something gorgeous anywhere you point a camera, especially under water. I took all of the underwater photos in this book with a simple compact Olympus TG-3. Post-processing in Lightroom and Photoshop.

In fact, *you don't even have to know how to swim to see most of the stuff from the snorkeling photos in this book.* Go chest-deep on a low tide in Moalboal, stick your head in the water to be amazed by corals and sardines. I don't dive; all of the UW photos are taken snorkeling no deeper than the depth of a swimming pool, 5'-20', although some of them are darkened for dramatic effect.

PERNILLA, DIVE INSTRUCTOR

MOALBOAL 2015

4

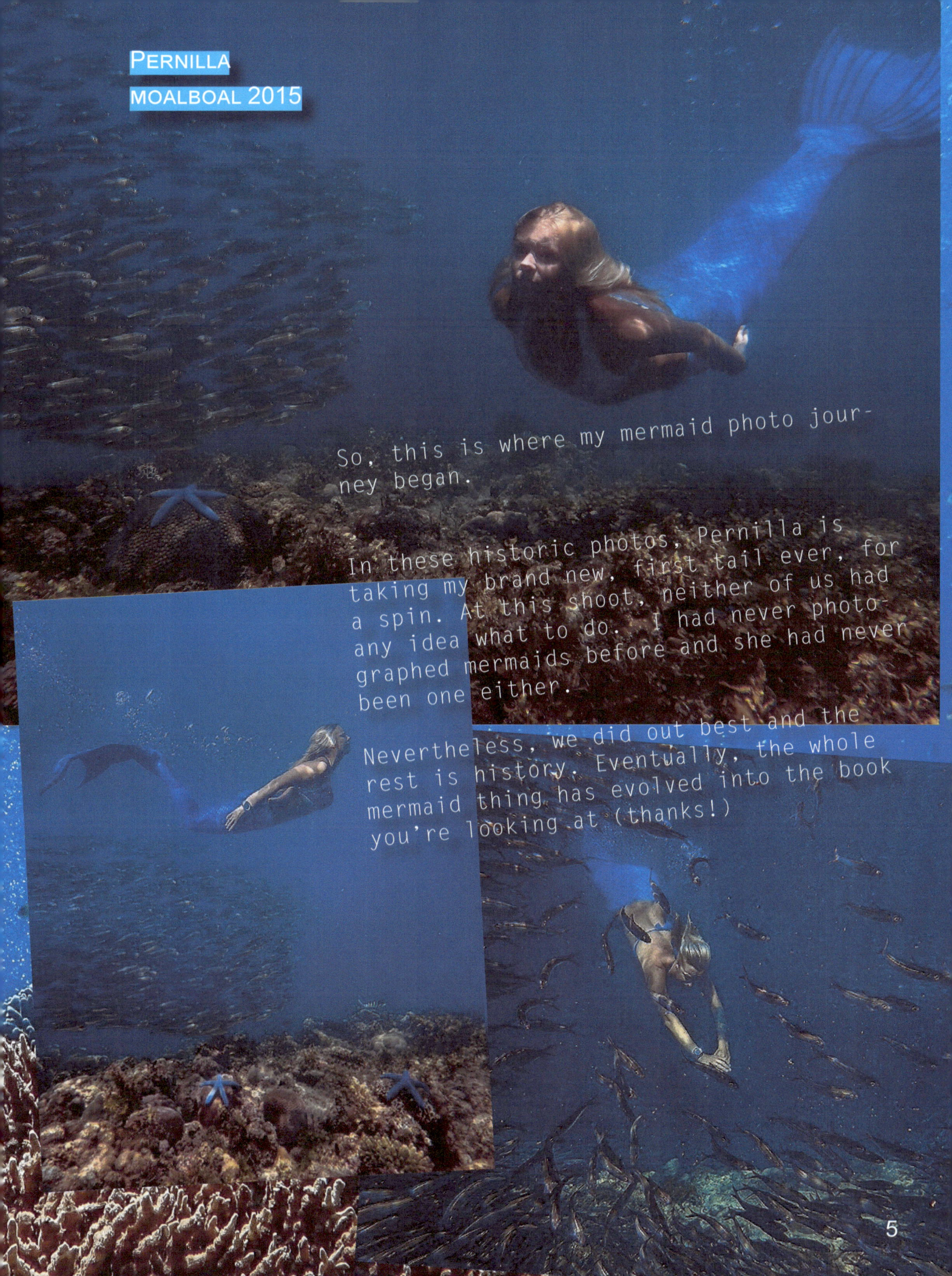

So, this is where my mermaid photo journey began.

In these historic photos, Pernilla is taking my brand new, first tail ever, for a spin. At this shoot, neither of us had any idea what to do. I had never photographed mermaids before and she had never been one either.

Nevertheless, we did out best and the rest is history. Eventually, the whole mermaid thing has evolved into the book you're looking at (thanks!)

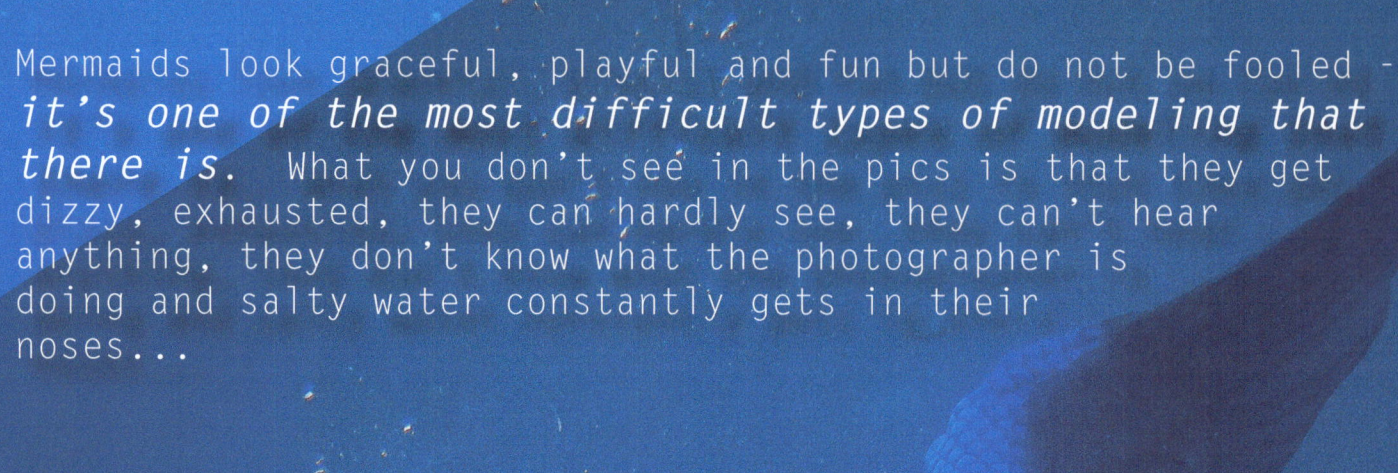

Mermaids look graceful, playful and fun but do not be fooled - *it's one of the most difficult types of modeling that there is.* What you don't see in the pics is that they get dizzy, exhausted, they can hardly see, they can't hear anything, they don't know what the photographer is doing and salty water constantly gets in their noses...

MERMAID: ROWENA

MOALBOAL 2015

...their feet are bound, striking the right pose takes several times longer under water because there is not really any communication with the photographer down there. It's very draining for both the photographer and the model but, of course, exhilarating and fun as well.

6

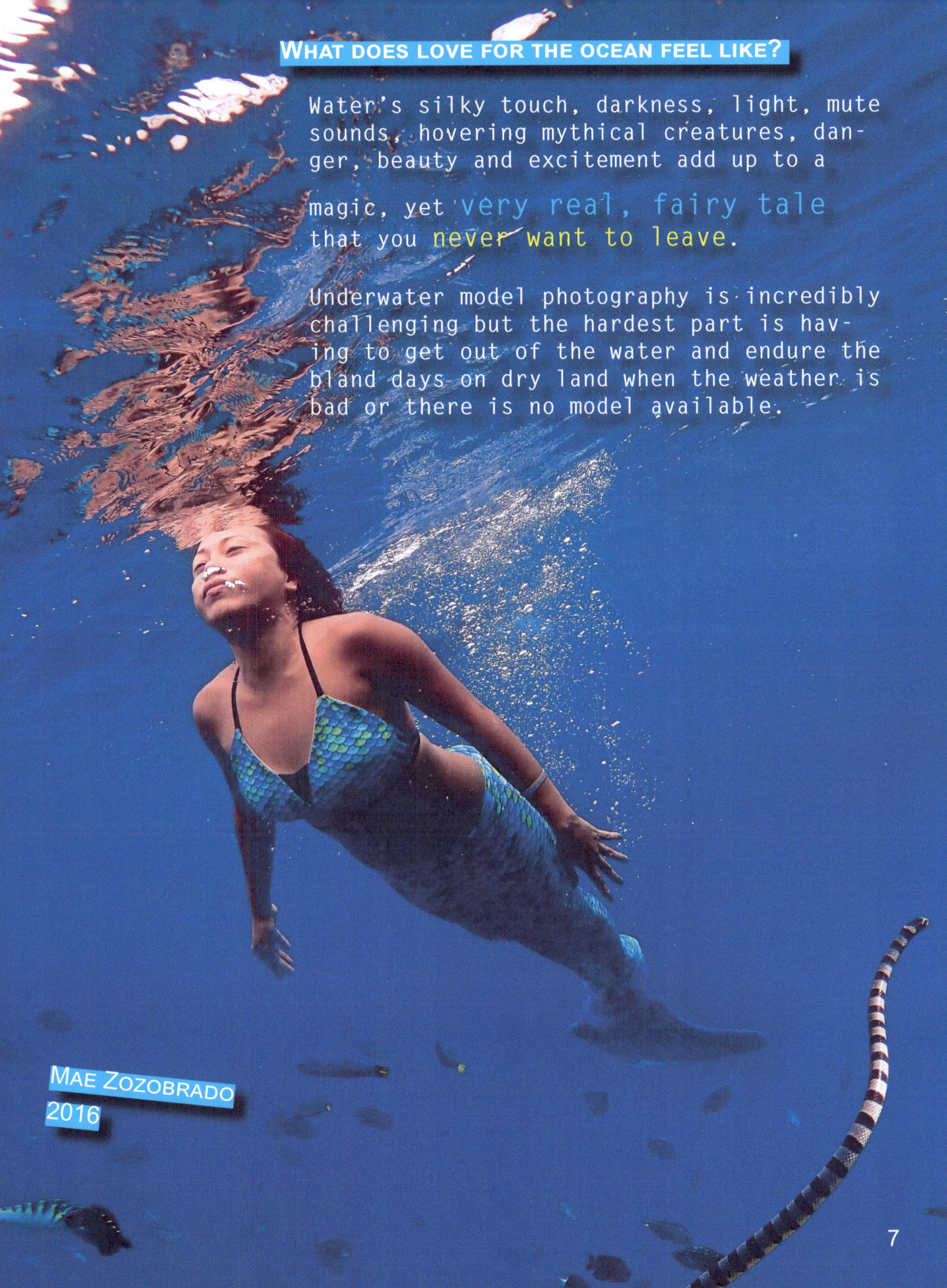

WHAT DOES LOVE FOR THE OCEAN FEEL LIKE?

Water's silky touch, darkness, light, mute sounds, hovering mythical creatures, danger, beauty and excitement add up to a

magic, yet very real, fairy tale that you never want to leave.

Underwater model photography is incredibly challenging but the hardest part is having to get out of the water and endure the bland days on dry land when the weather is bad or there is no model available.

MAE ZOZOBRADO
2016

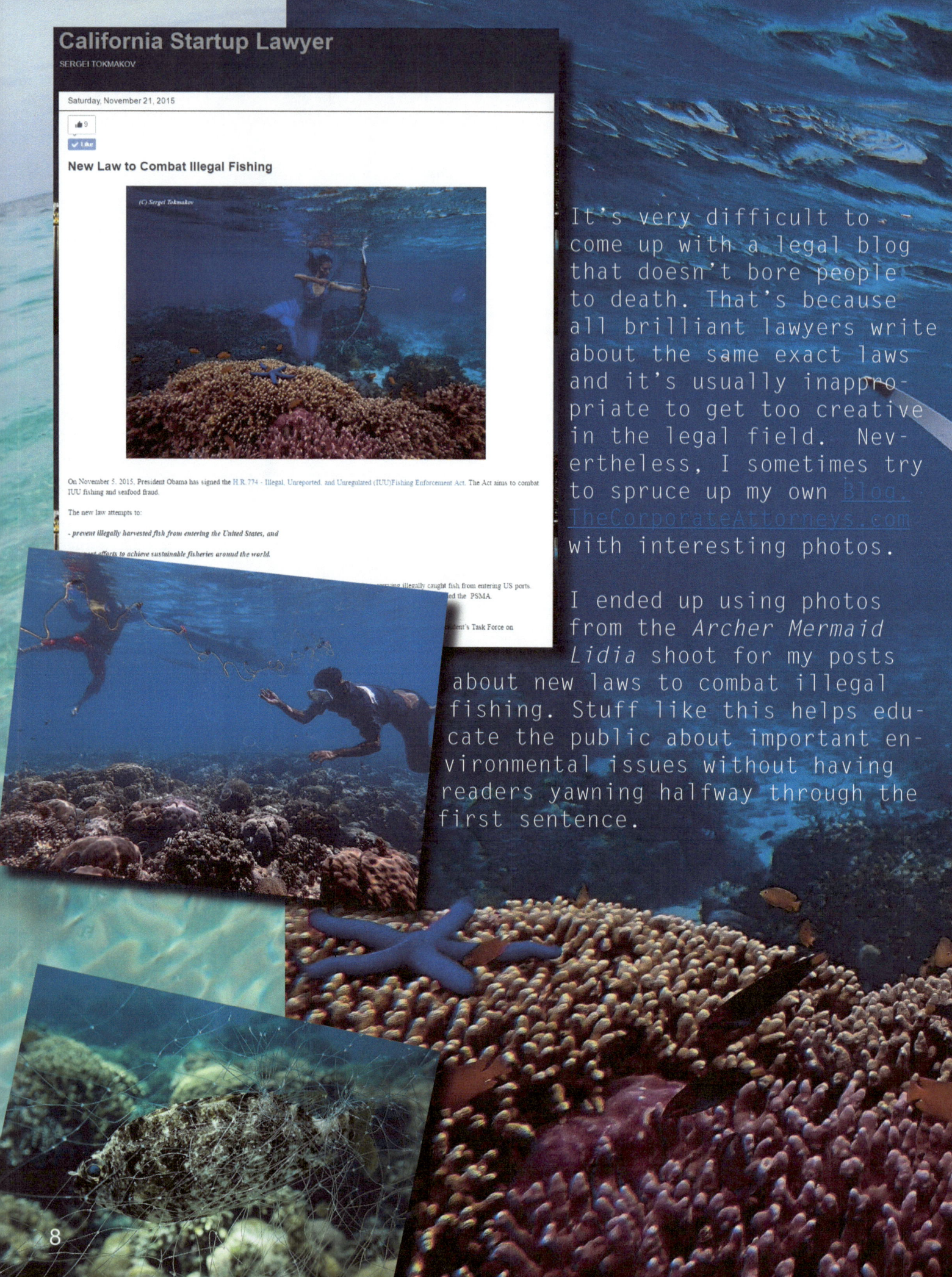

California Startup Lawyer
SERGEI TOKMAKOV

Saturday, November 21, 2015

👍 9

✔ Like

New Law to Combat Illegal Fishing

(C) Sergei Tokmakov

On November 5, 2015, President Obama has signed the H.R. 774 - Illegal, Unreported, and Unregulated (IUU) Fishing Enforcement Act. The Act aims to combat IUU fishing and seafood fraud.

The new law attempts to:

- *prevent illegally harvested fish from entering the United States, and*

...ent efforts to achieve sustainable fisheries around the world.

...rying illegally caught fish from entering US ports.
...ed the PSMA.

...dent's Task Force on

It's very difficult to come up with a legal blog that doesn't bore people to death. That's because all brilliant lawyers write about the same exact laws and it's usually inappropriate to get too creative in the legal field. Nevertheless, I sometimes try to spruce up my own Blog. TheCorporateAttorneys.com with interesting photos.

I ended up using photos from the *Archer Mermaid Lidia* shoot for my posts about new laws to combat illegal fishing. Stuff like this helps educate the public about important environmental issues without having readers yawning halfway through the first sentence.

8

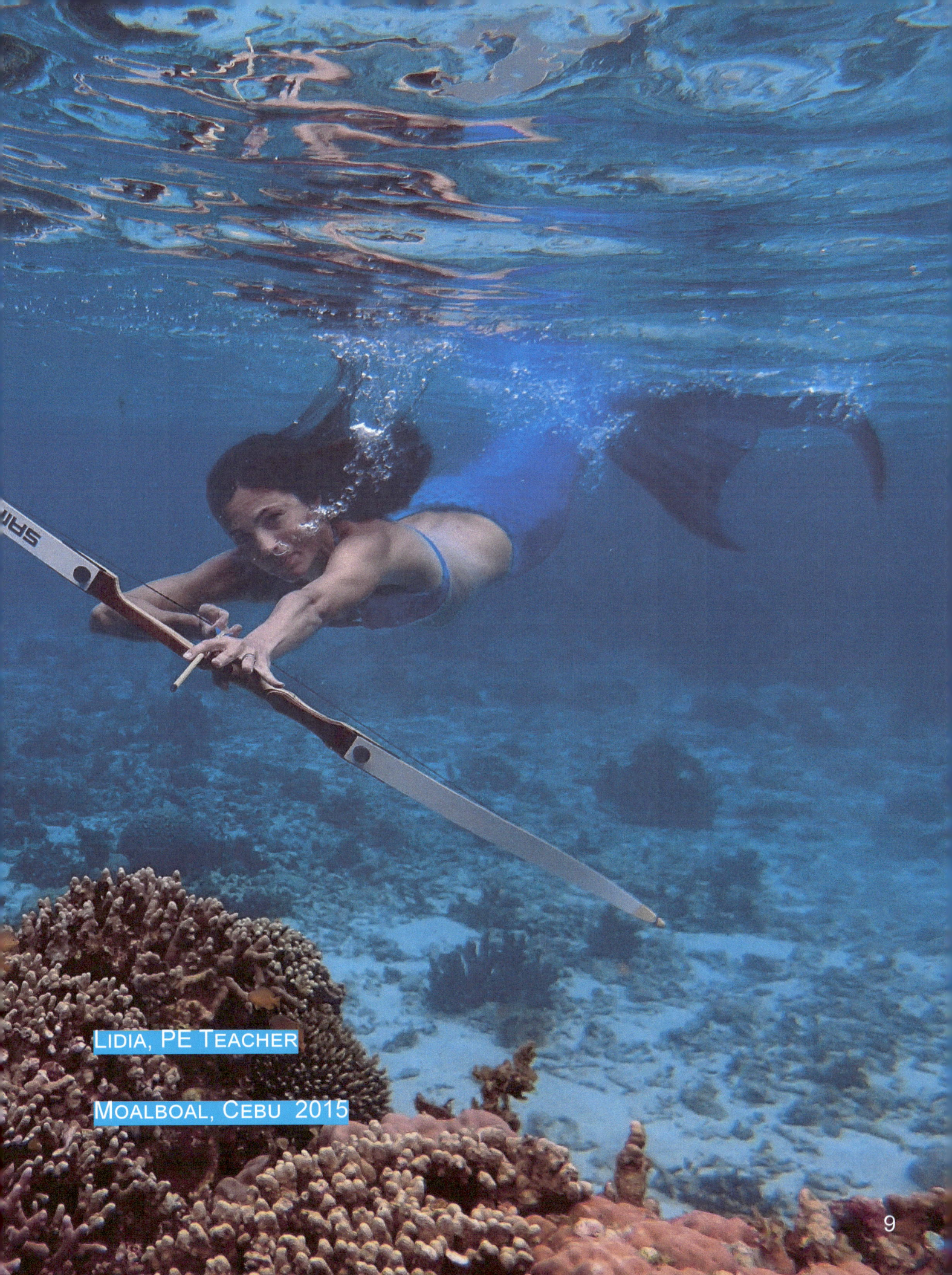

LIDIA, PE TEACHER

MOALBOAL, CEBU 2015

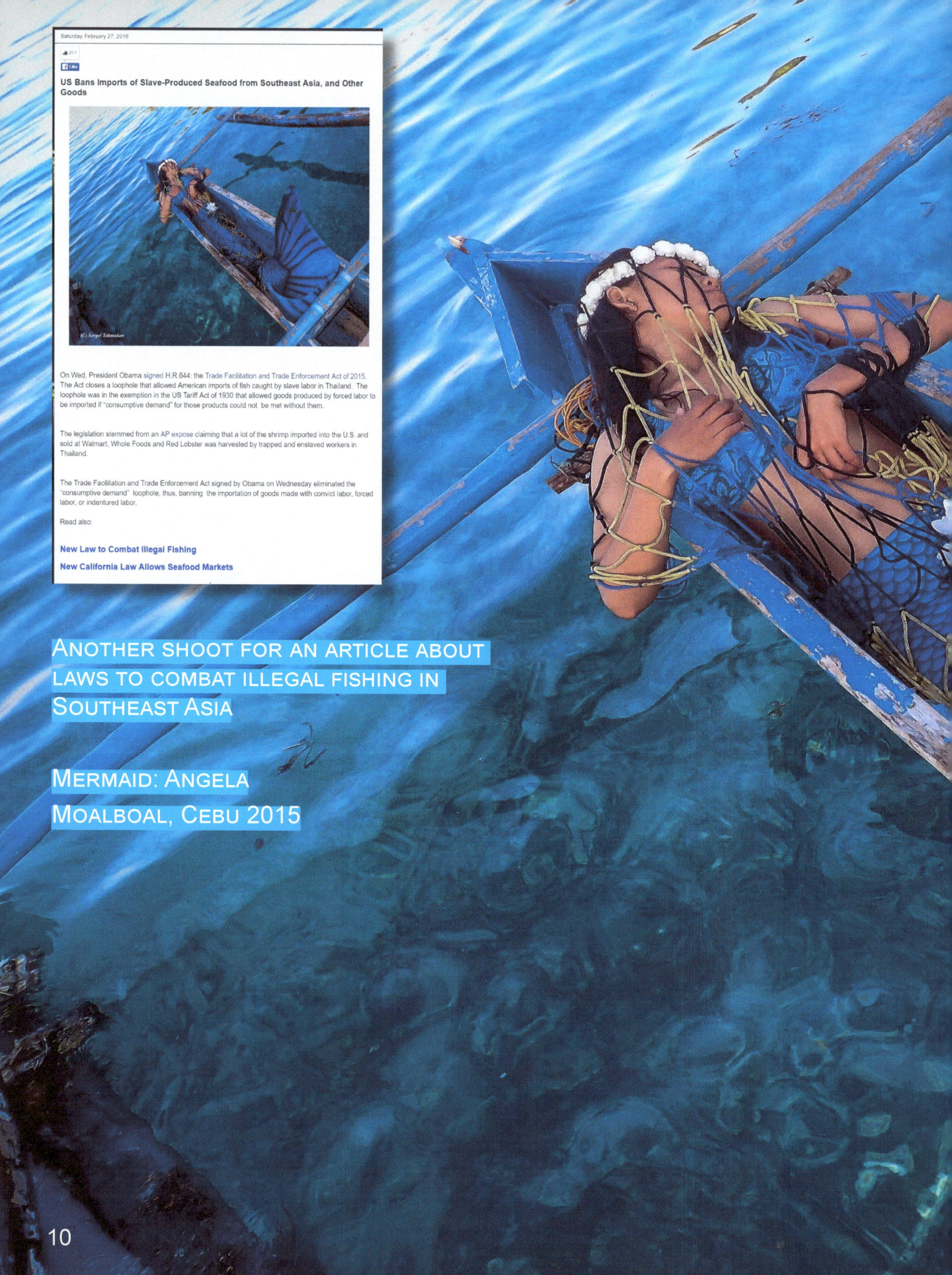

ANOTHER SHOOT FOR AN ARTICLE ABOUT LAWS TO COMBAT ILLEGAL FISHING IN SOUTHEAST ASIA

MERMAID: ANGELA
MOALBOAL, CEBU 2015

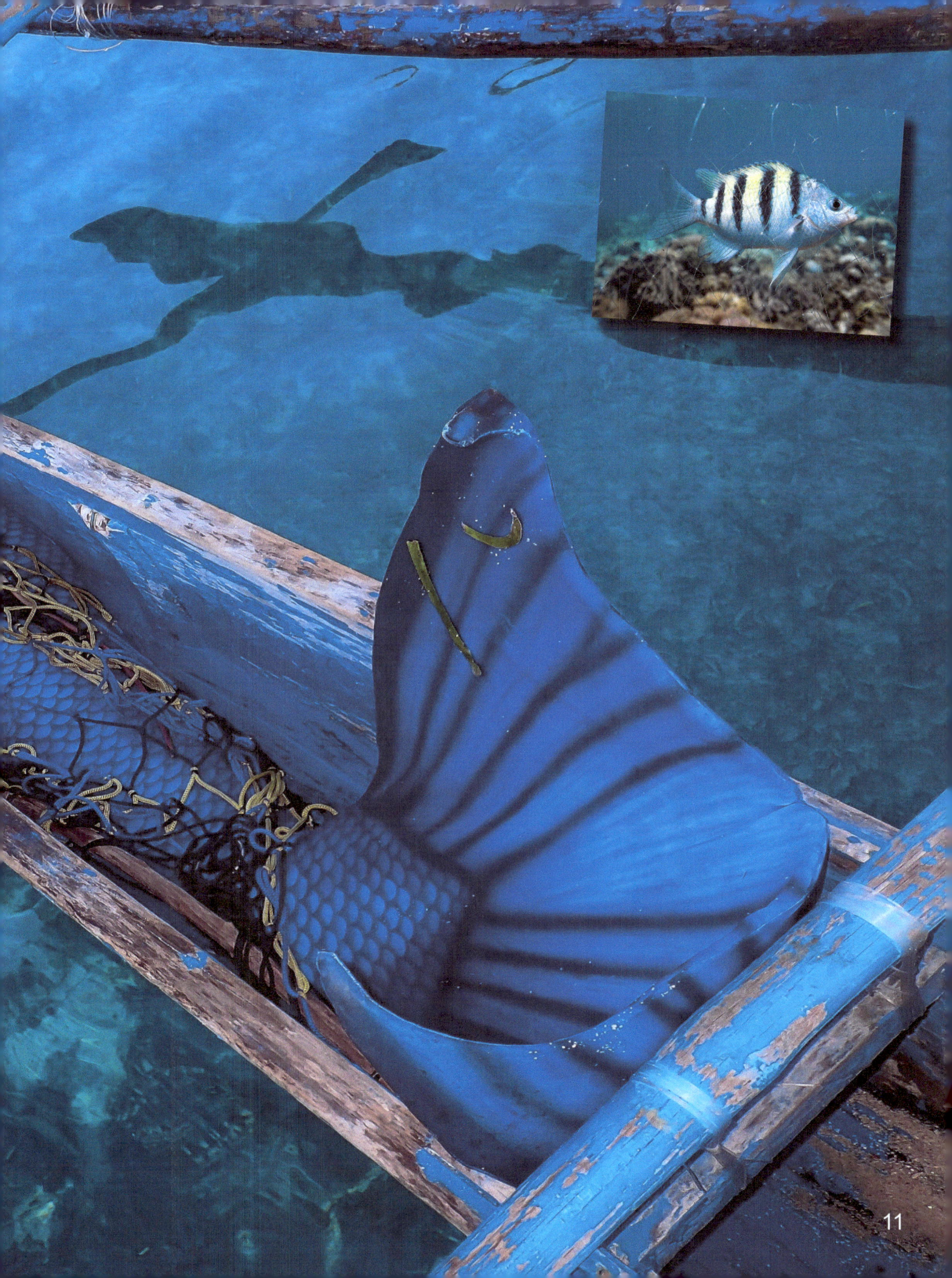

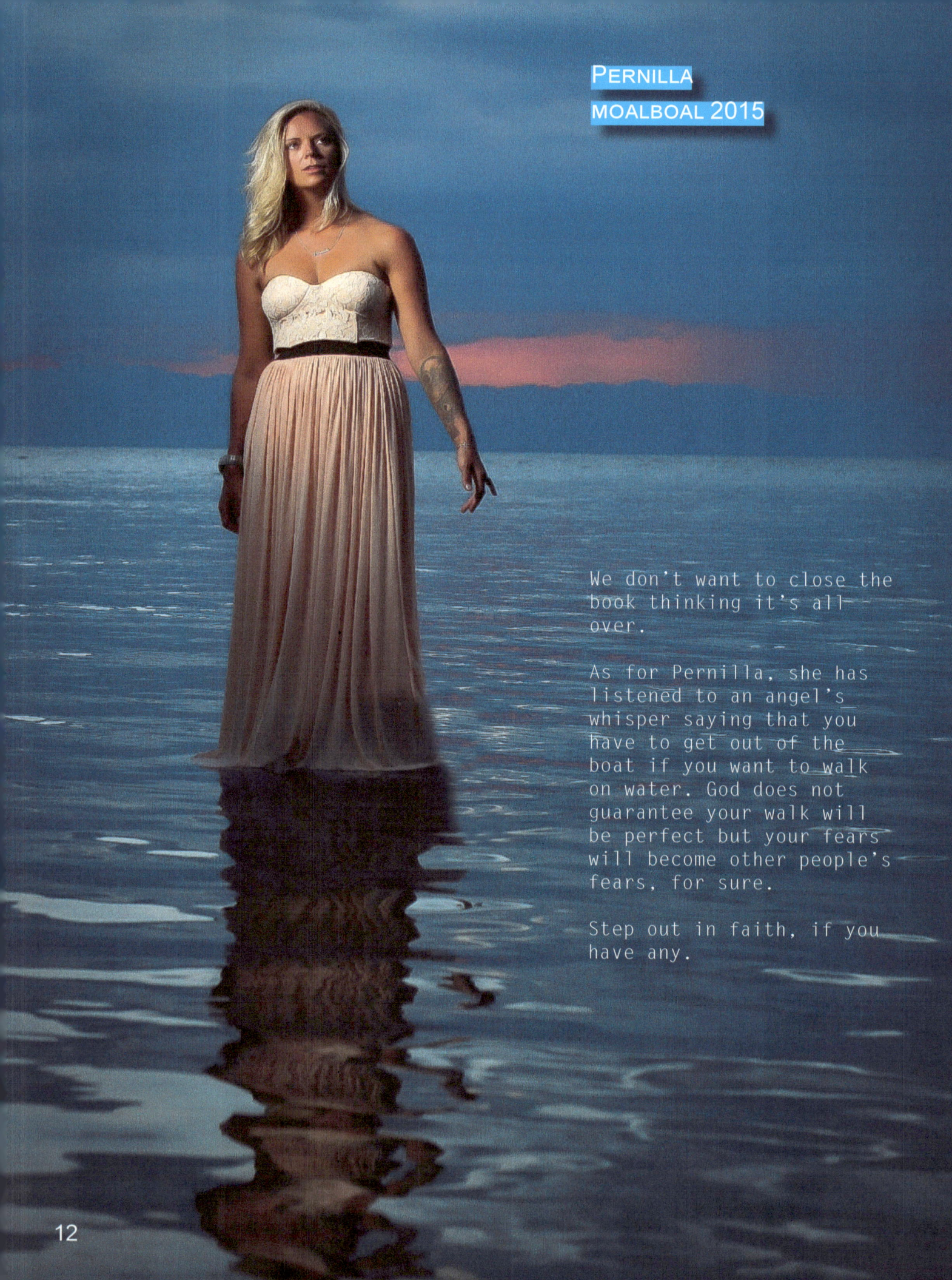

PERNILLA
MOALBOAL 2015

We don't want to close the book thinking it's all over.

As for Pernilla, she has listened to an angel's whisper saying that you have to get out of the boat if you want to walk on water. God does not guarantee your walk will be perfect but your fears will become other people's fears, for sure.

Step out in faith, if you have any.

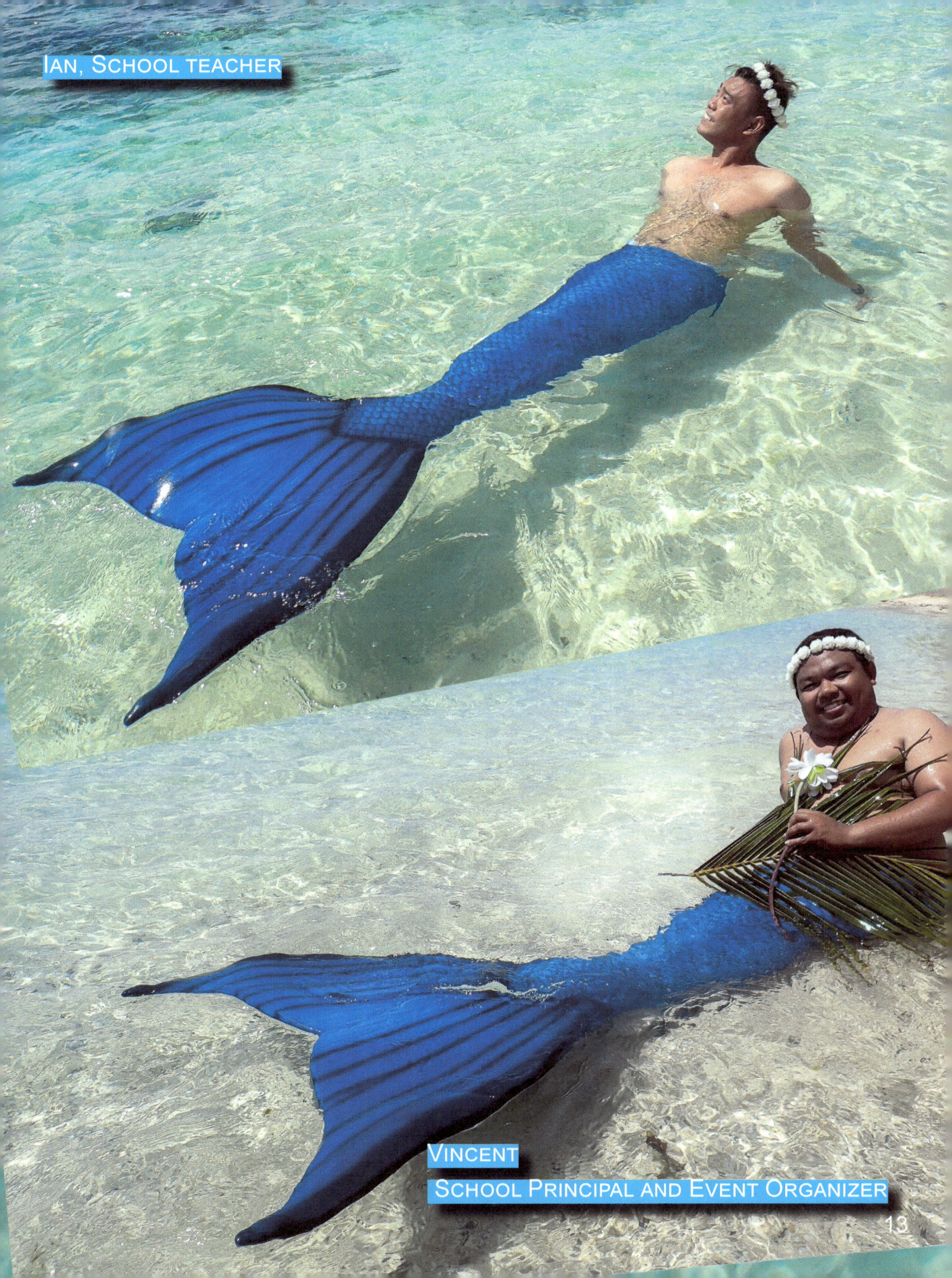

IAN, SCHOOL TEACHER

VINCENT
SCHOOL PRINCIPAL AND EVENT ORGANIZER

13

Starting over, starting fresh
- one of those moments in life
when falling still feels like
flying but you know that ulti-
mately everything is going to
be okay.

The future starts today.

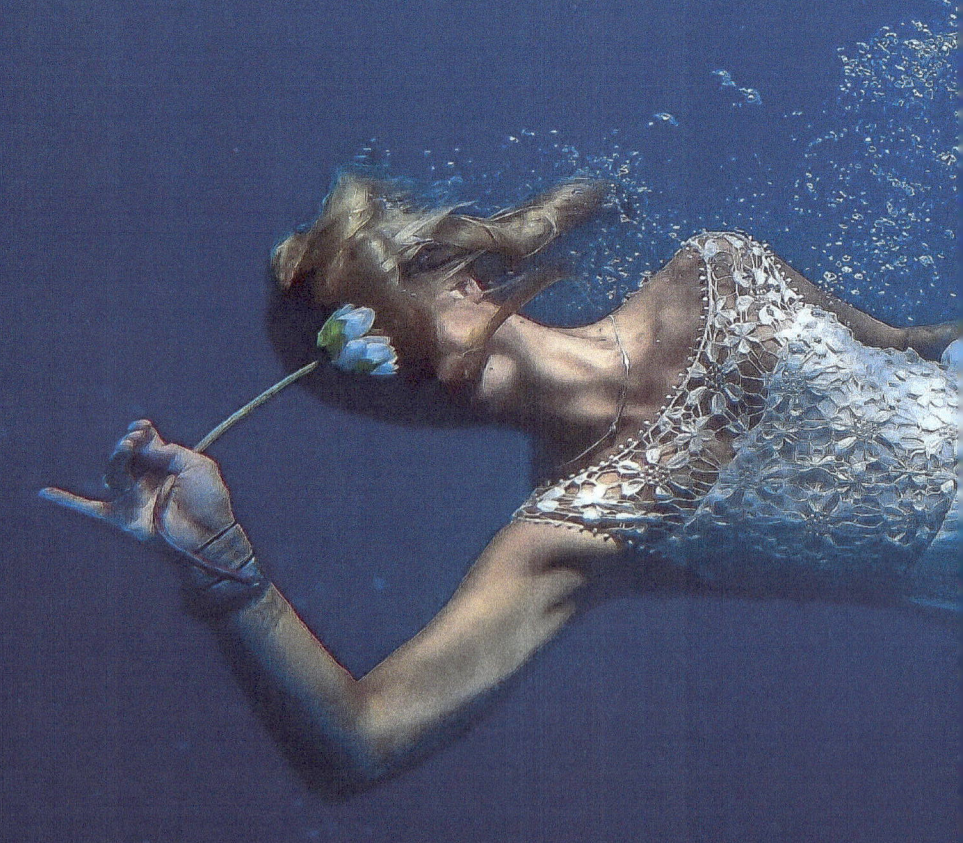

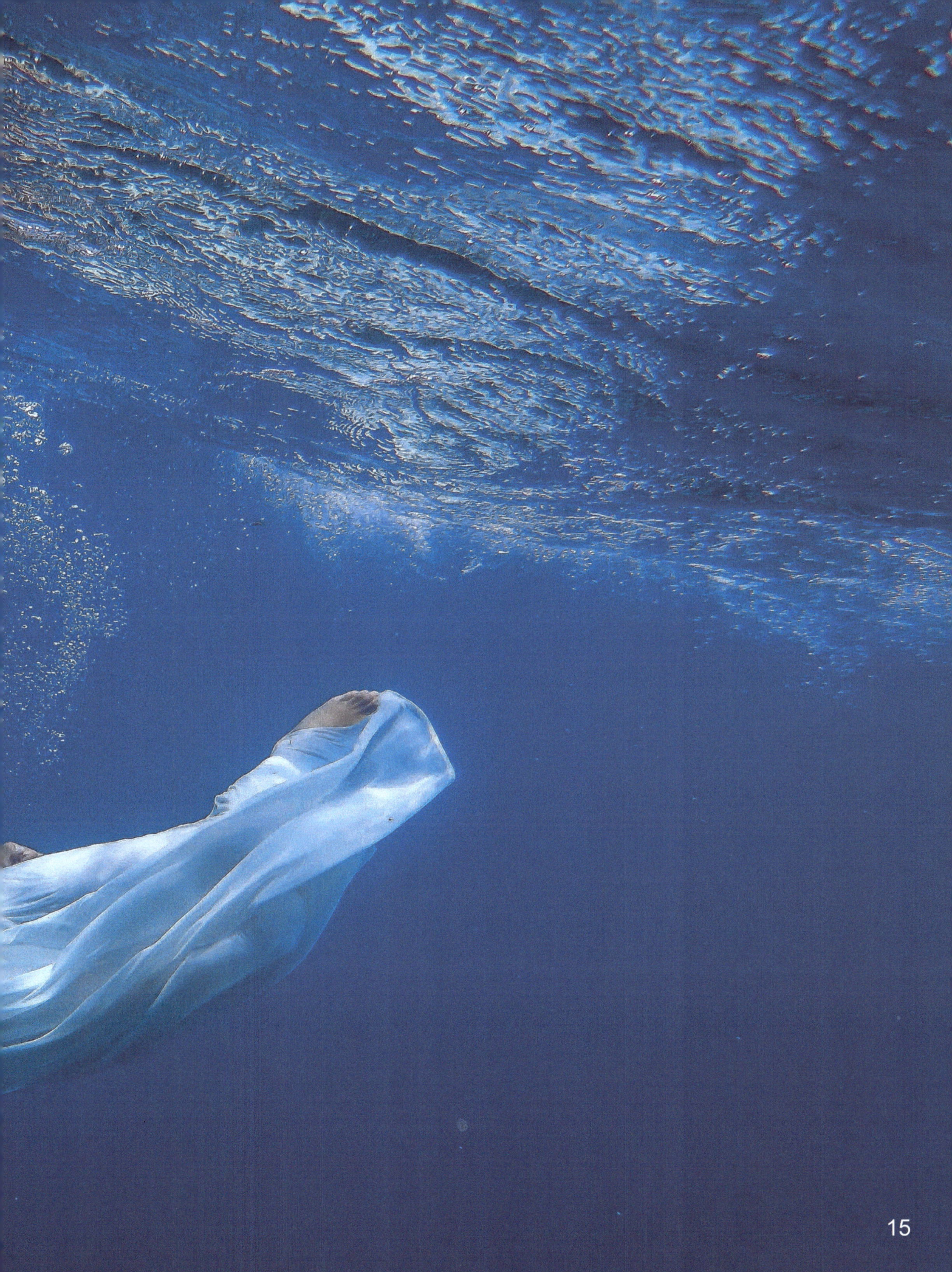

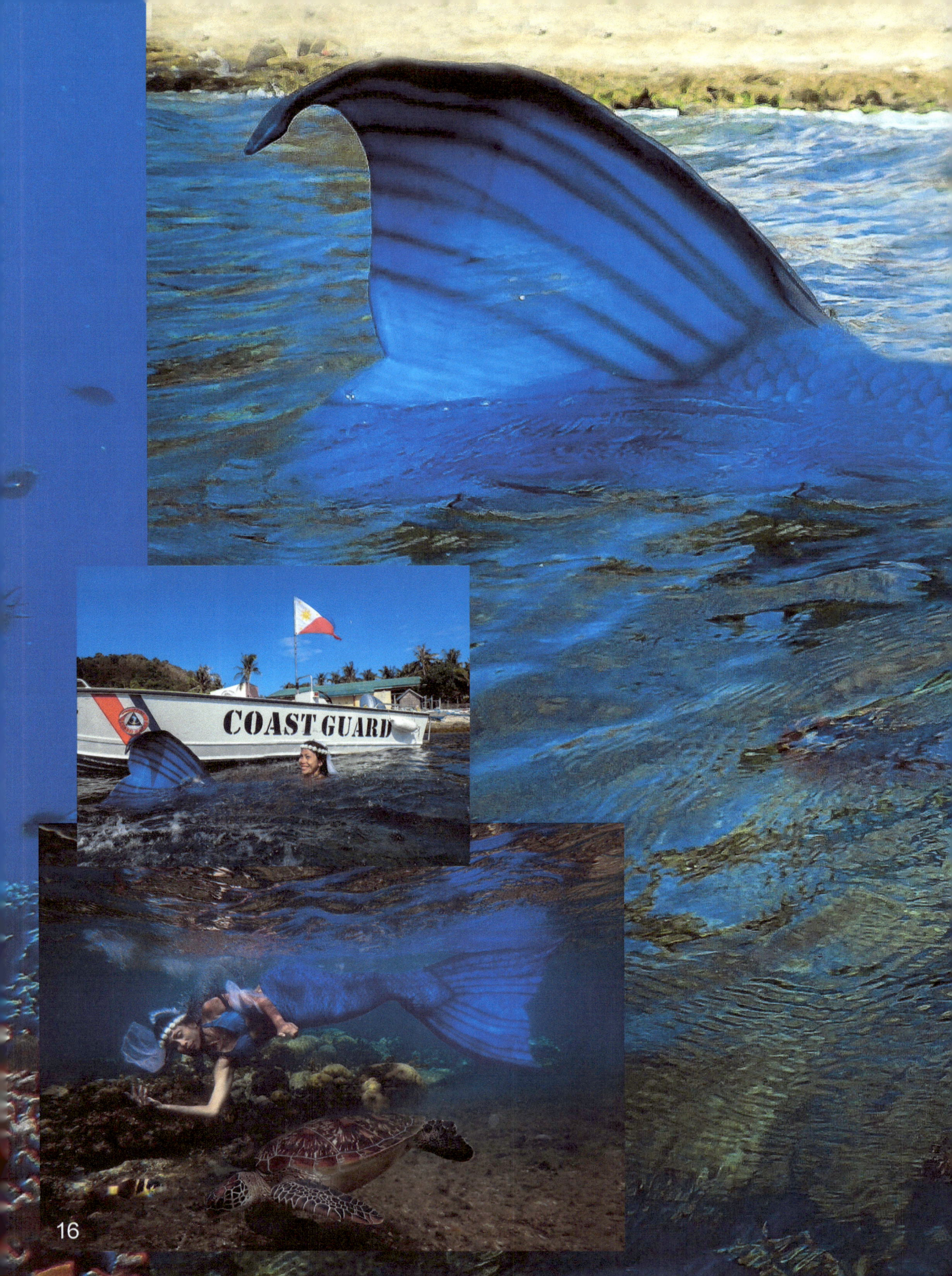

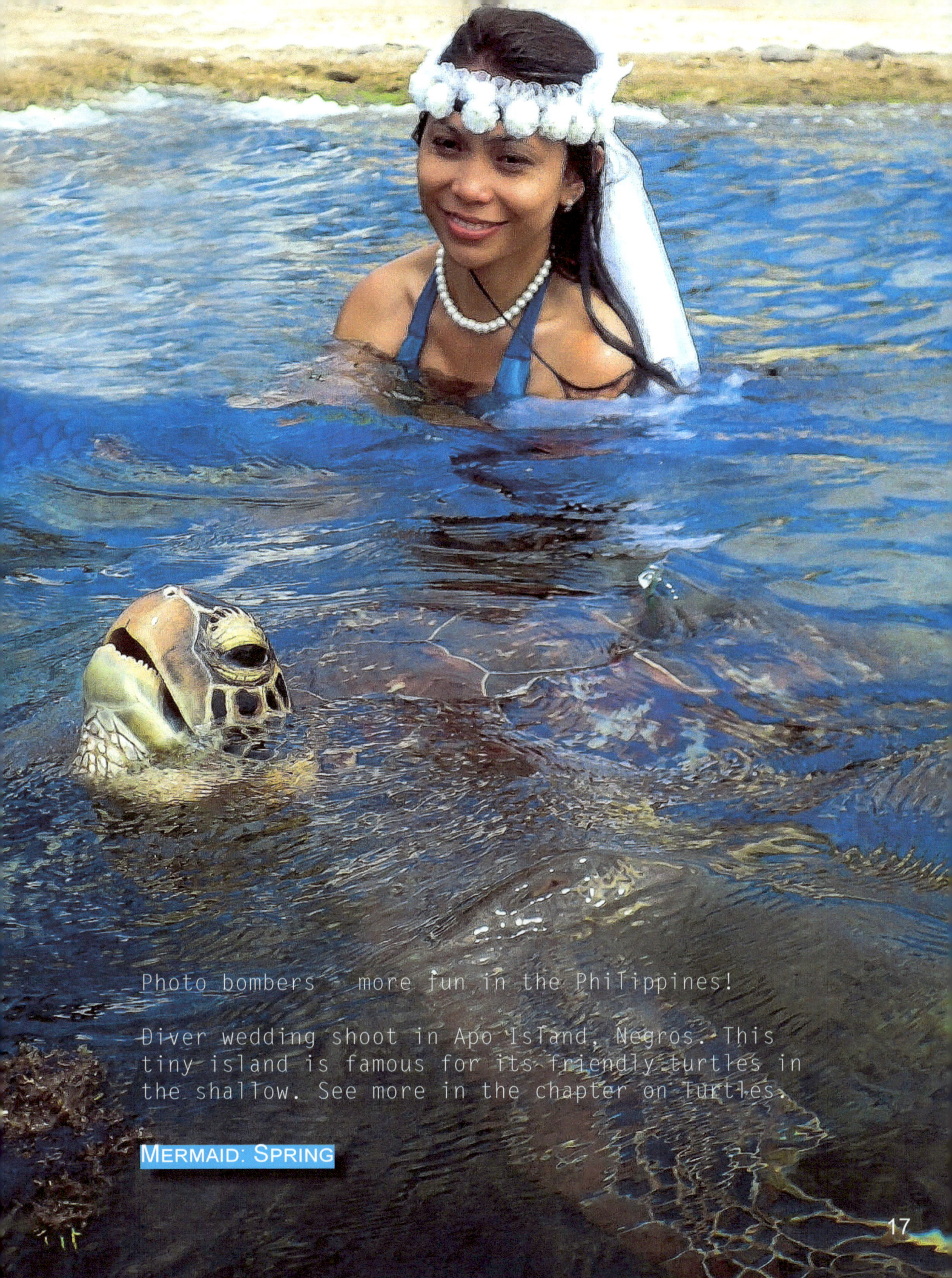

Photo bombers — more fun in the Philippines!

Diver wedding shoot in Apo Island, Negros. This tiny island is famous for its friendly turtles in the shallow. See more in the chapter on Turtles.

MERMAID: SPRING

17

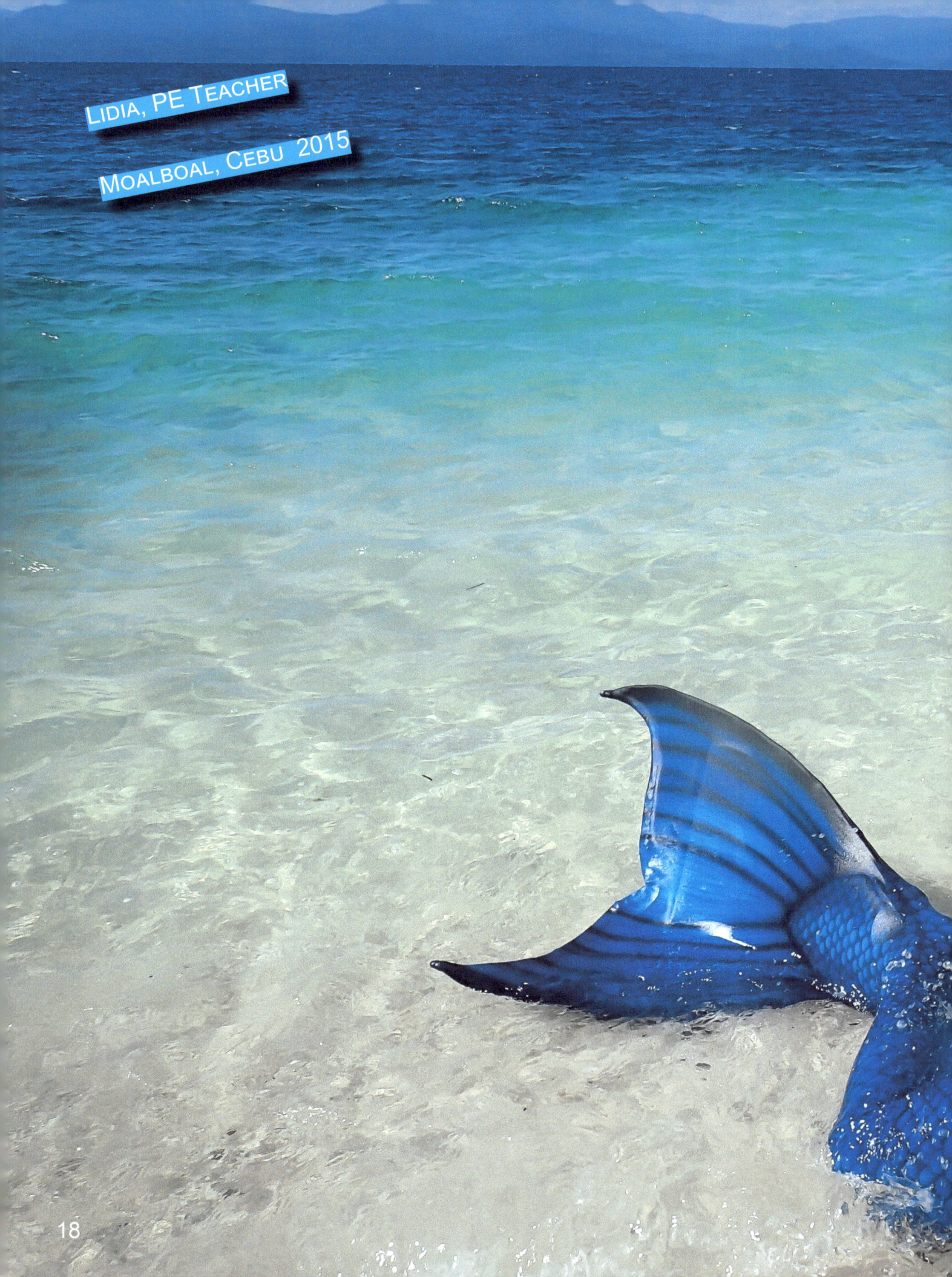

LIDIA, PE TEACHER

MOALBOAL, CEBU 2015

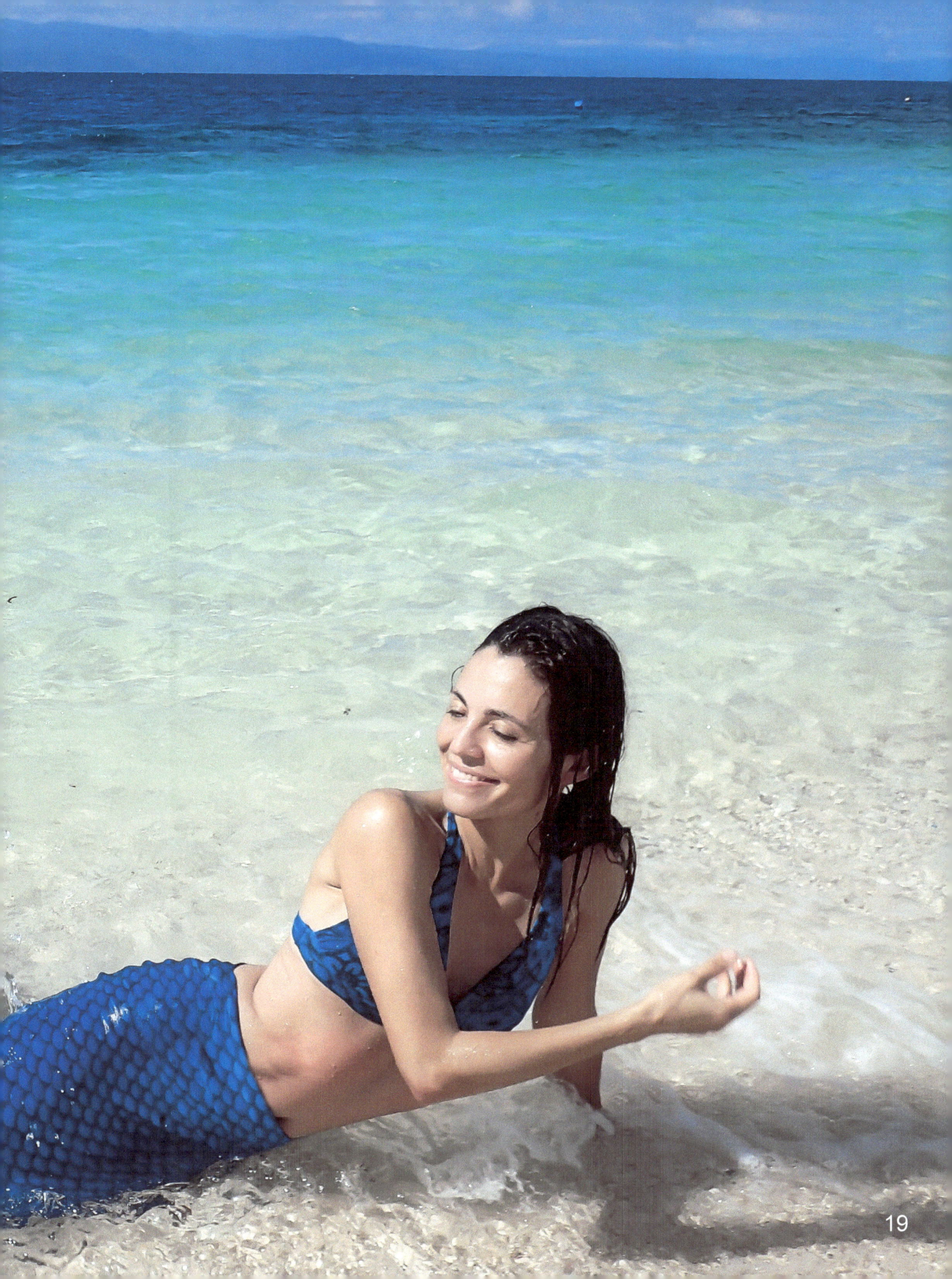

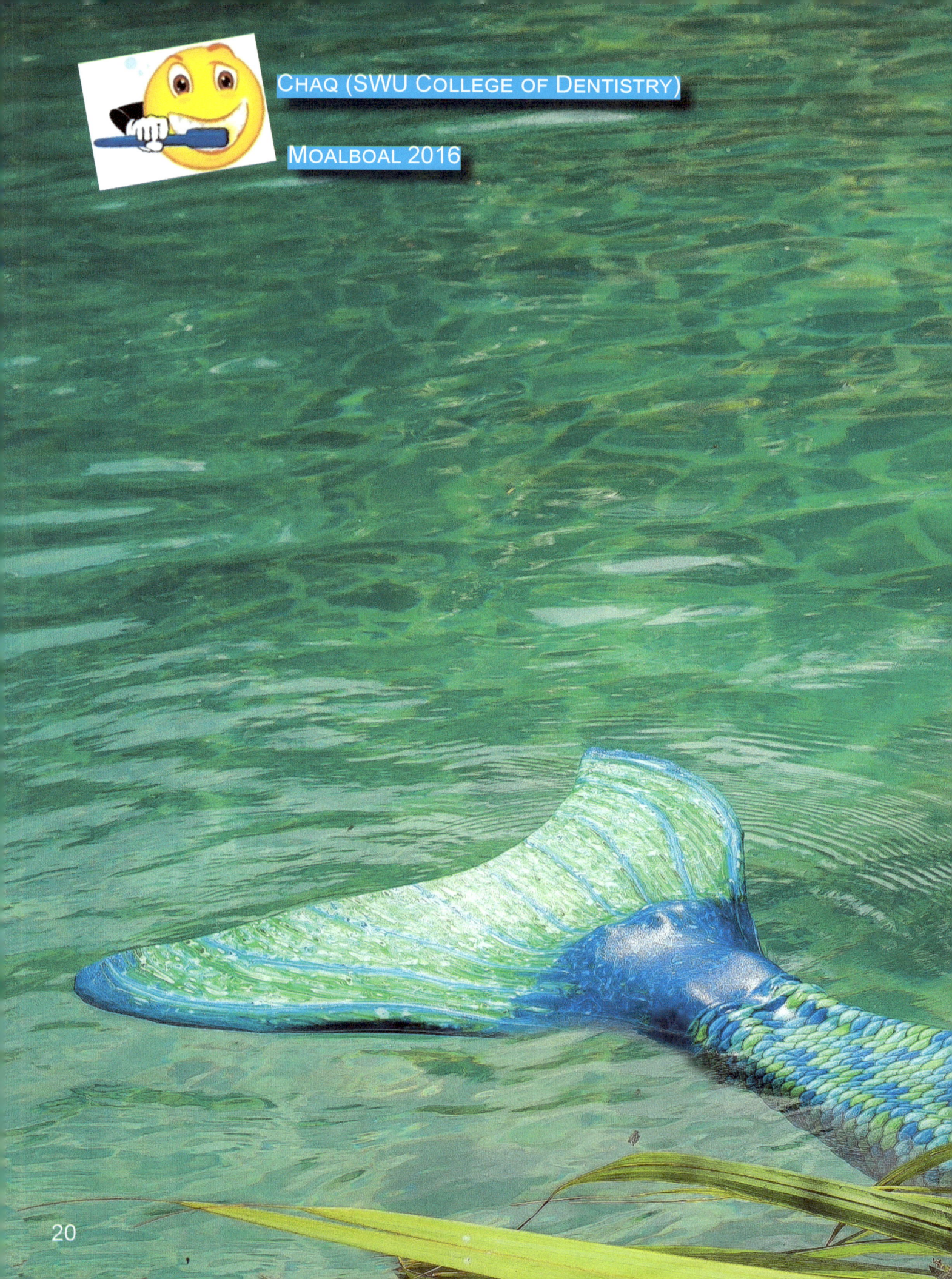

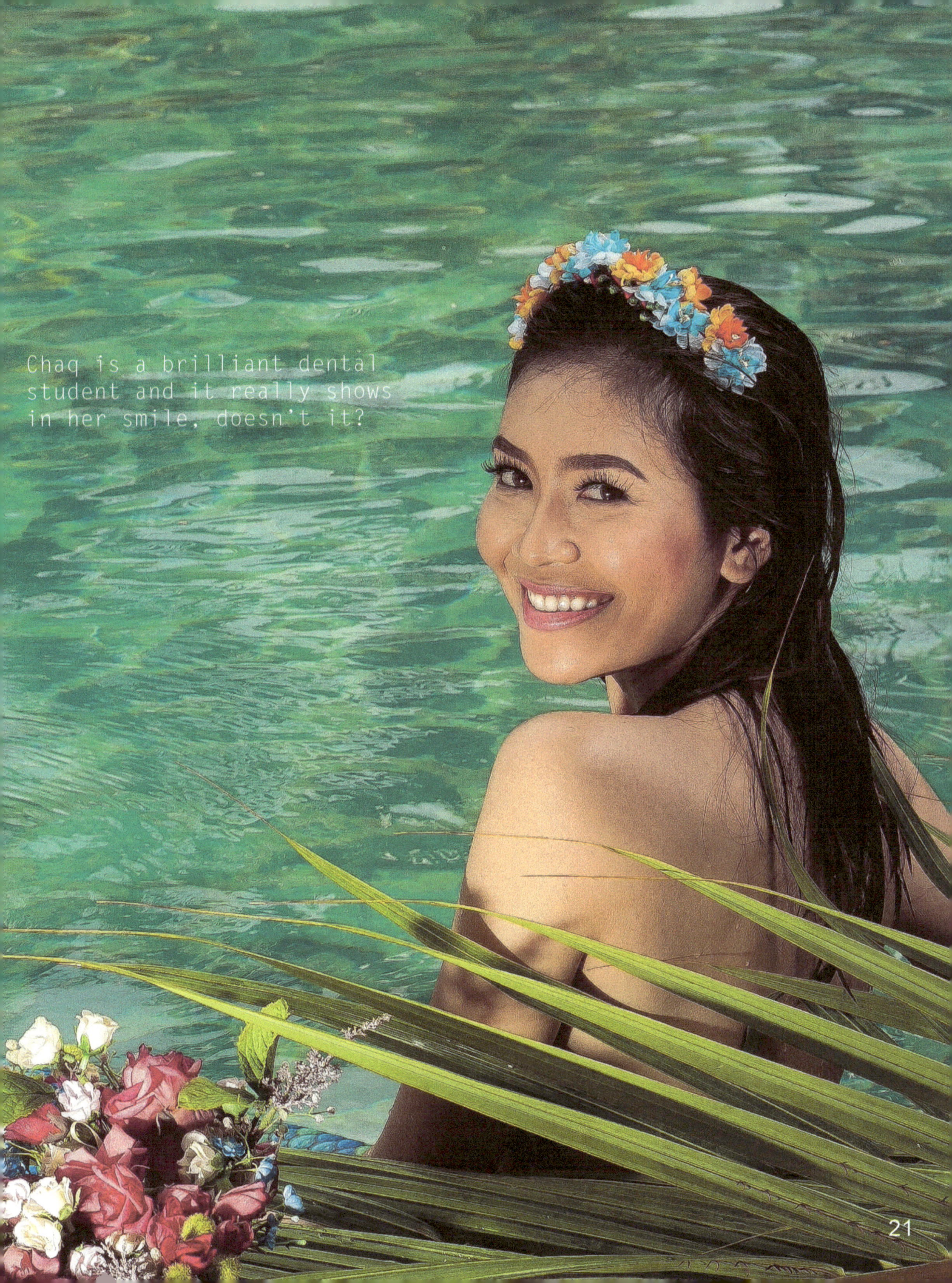

Chaq is a brilliant dental student and it really shows in her smile, doesn't it?

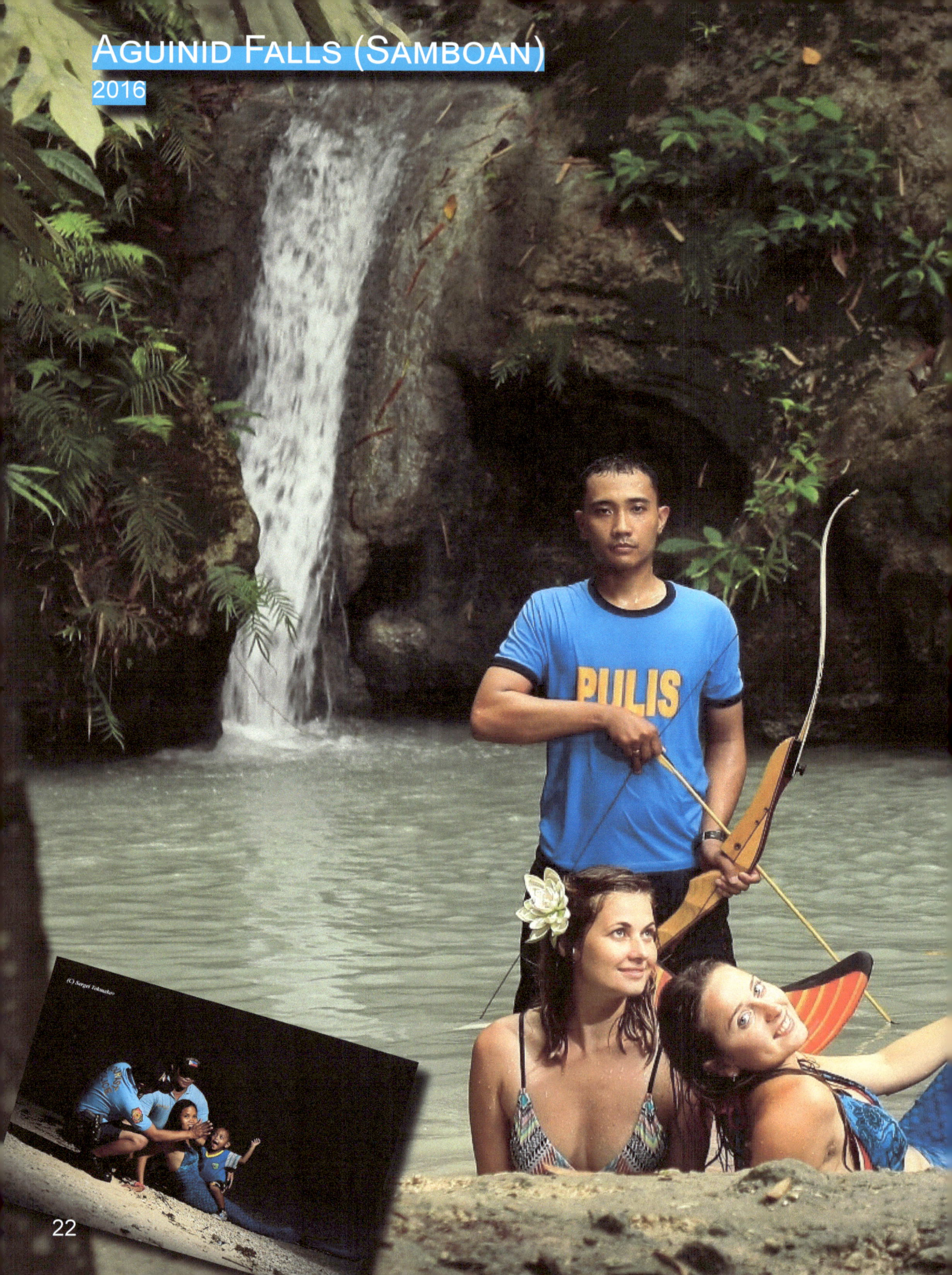

(C) Sergei Tokmakov

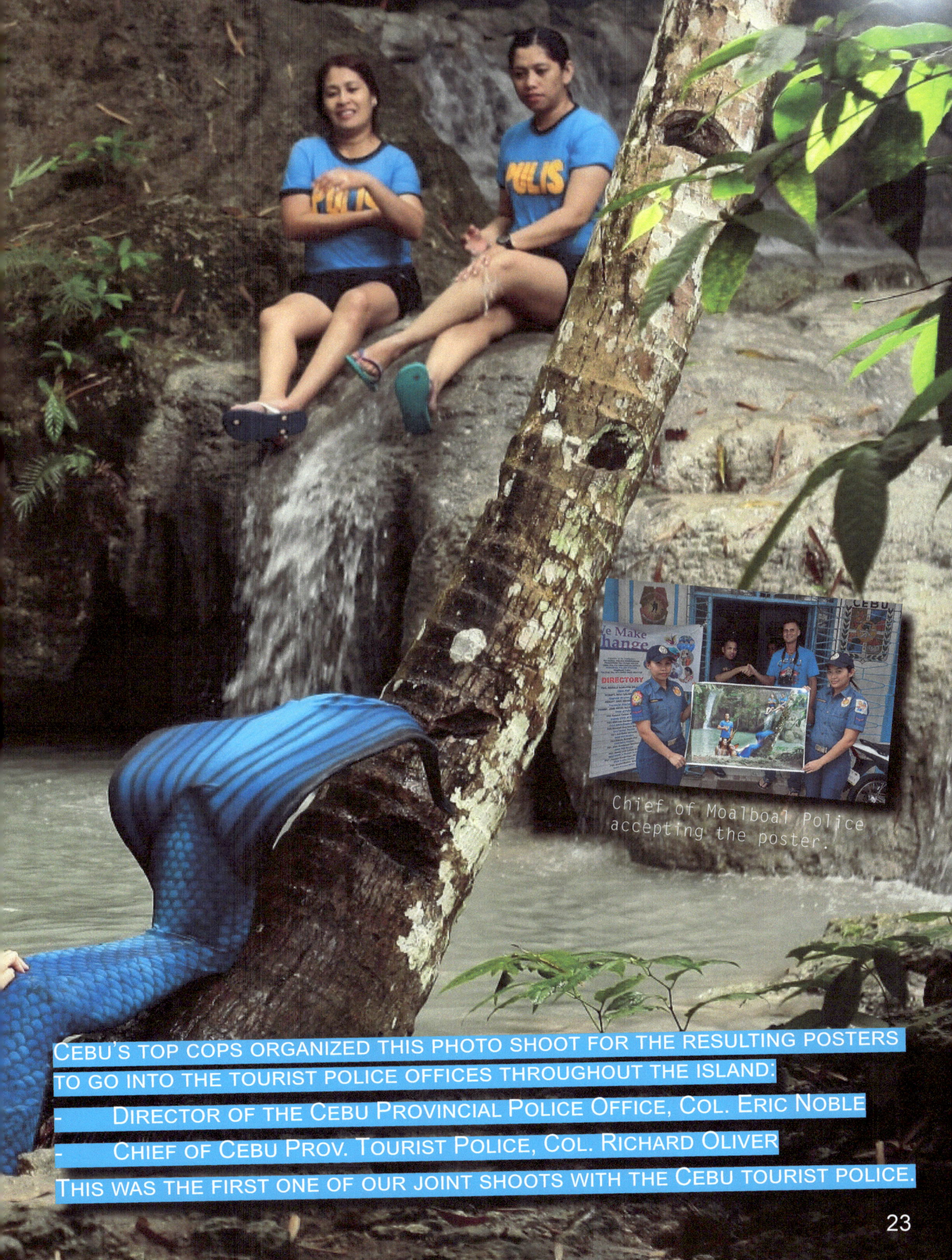

Chief of Moalboal Police
accepting the poster.

CEBU'S TOP COPS ORGANIZED THIS PHOTO SHOOT FOR THE RESULTING POSTERS TO GO INTO THE TOURIST POLICE OFFICES THROUGHOUT THE ISLAND:
- DIRECTOR OF THE CEBU PROVINCIAL POLICE OFFICE, COL. ERIC NOBLE
- CHIEF OF CEBU PROV. TOURIST POLICE, COL. RICHARD OLIVER
THIS WAS THE FIRST ONE OF OUR JOINT SHOOTS WITH THE CEBU TOURIST POLICE.

23

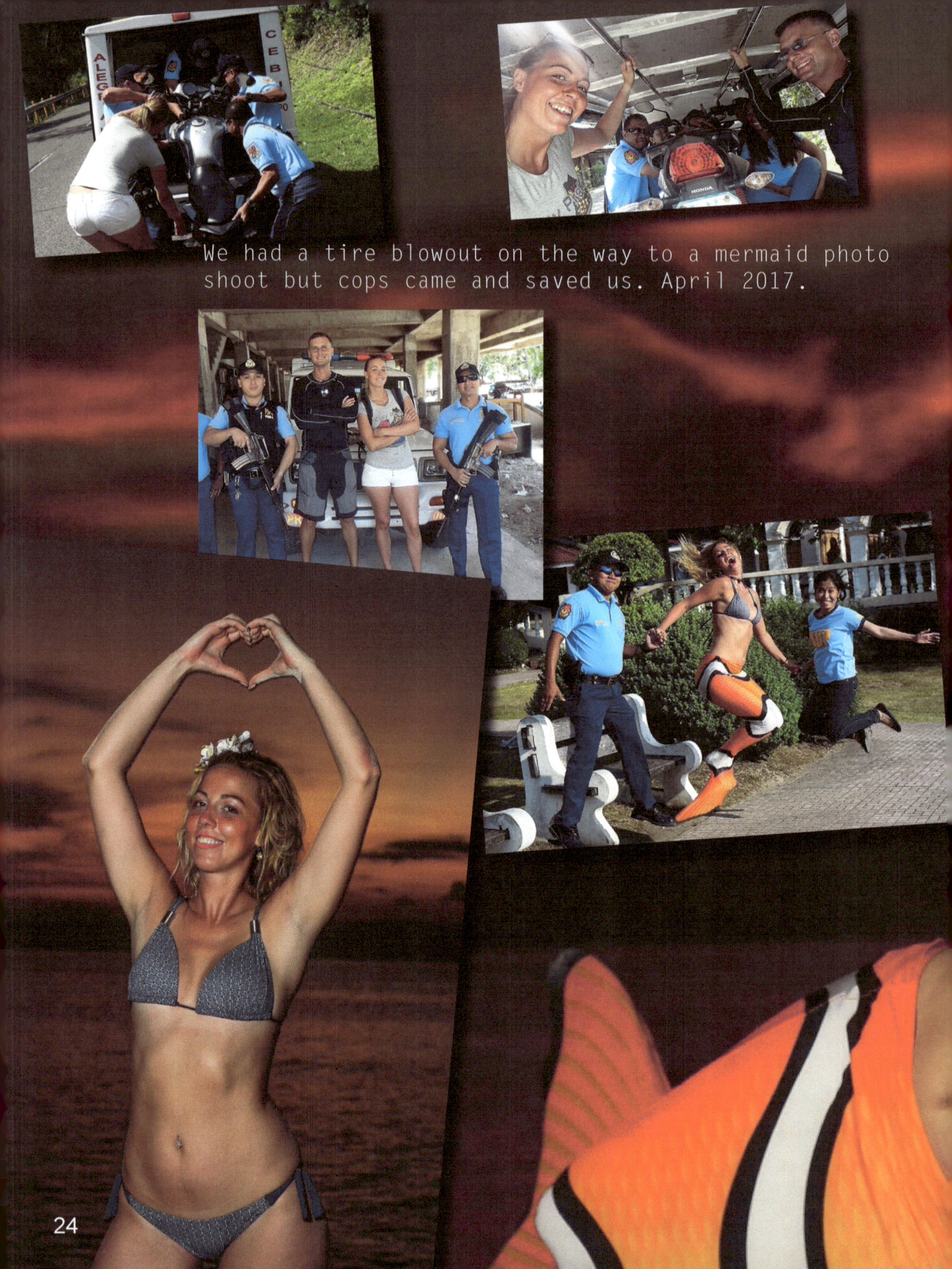

We had a tire blowout on the way to a mermaid photo shoot but cops came and saved us. April 2017.

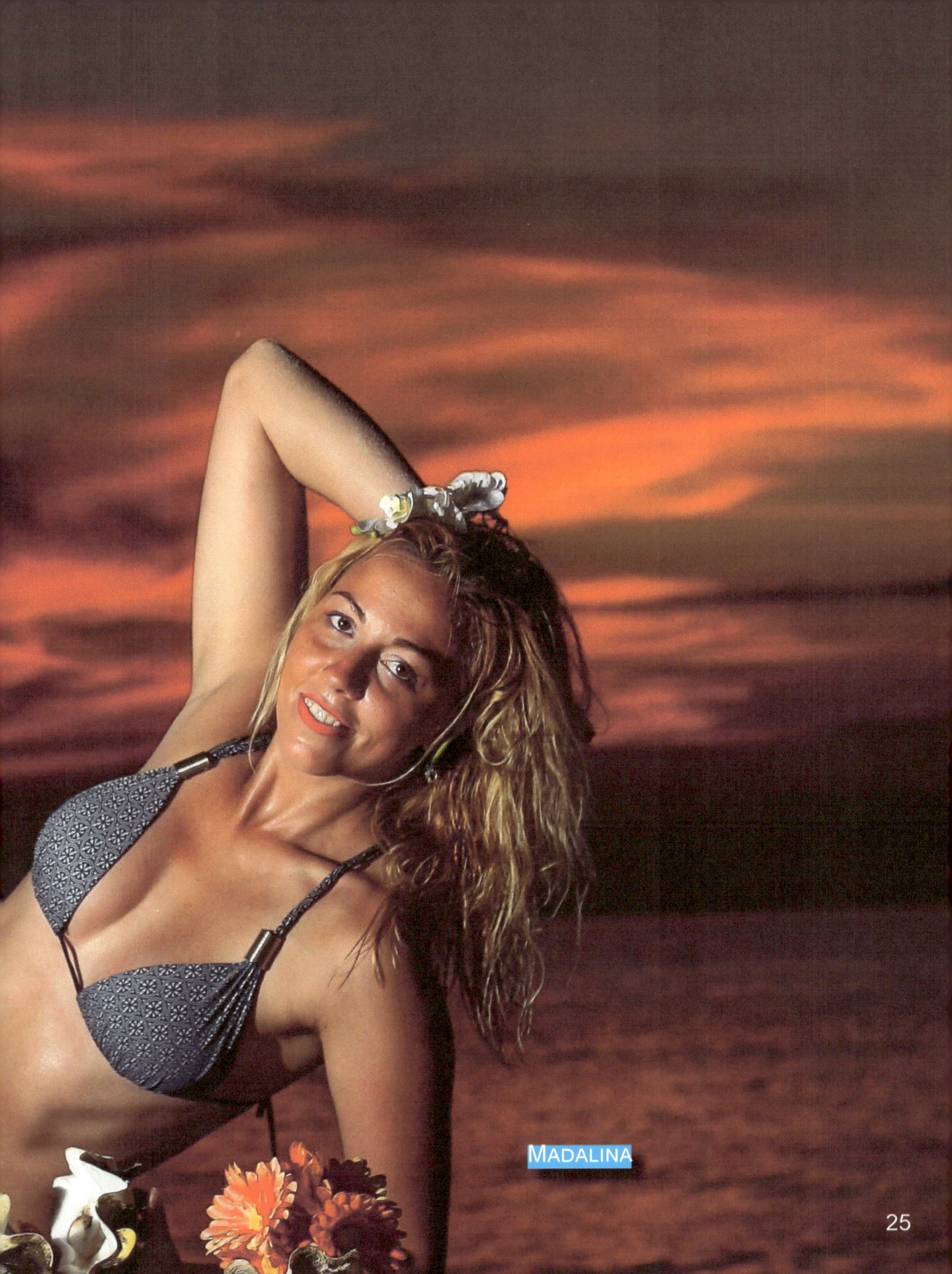

MADALINA

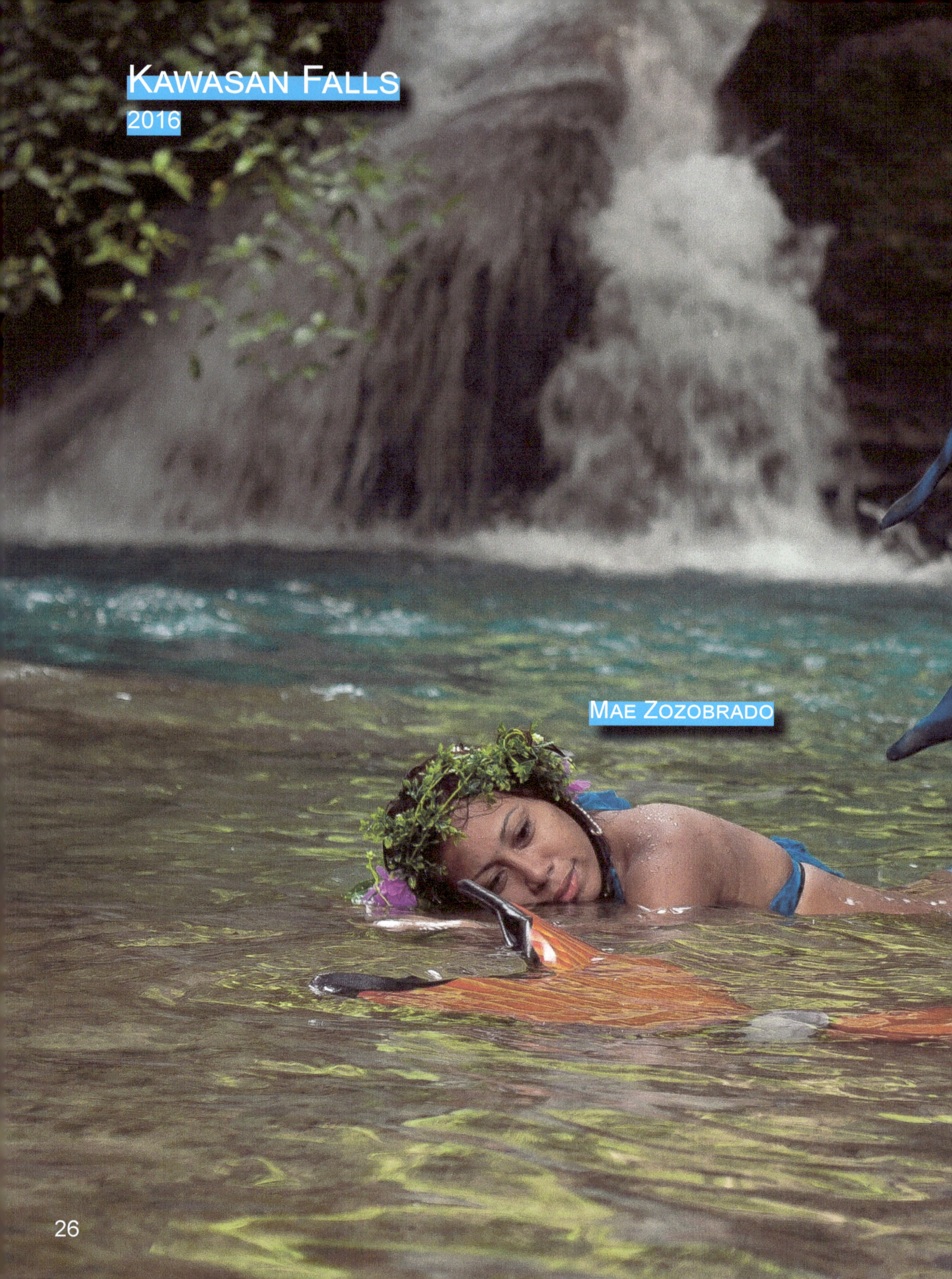

Kawasan Falls
2016

Mae Zozobrado

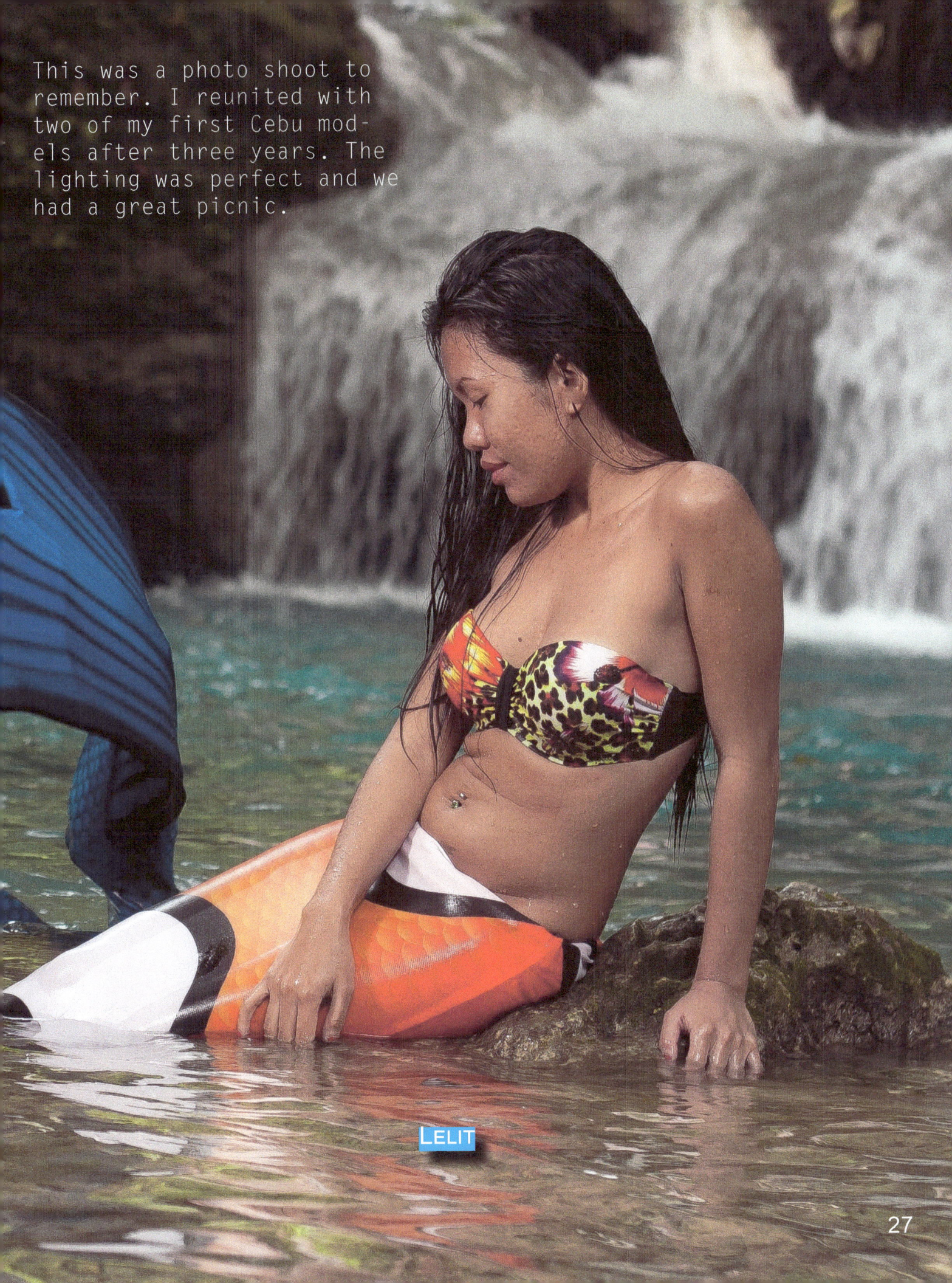

This was a photo shoot to remember. I reunited with two of my first Cebu models after three years. The lighting was perfect and we had a great picnic.

LELIT

27

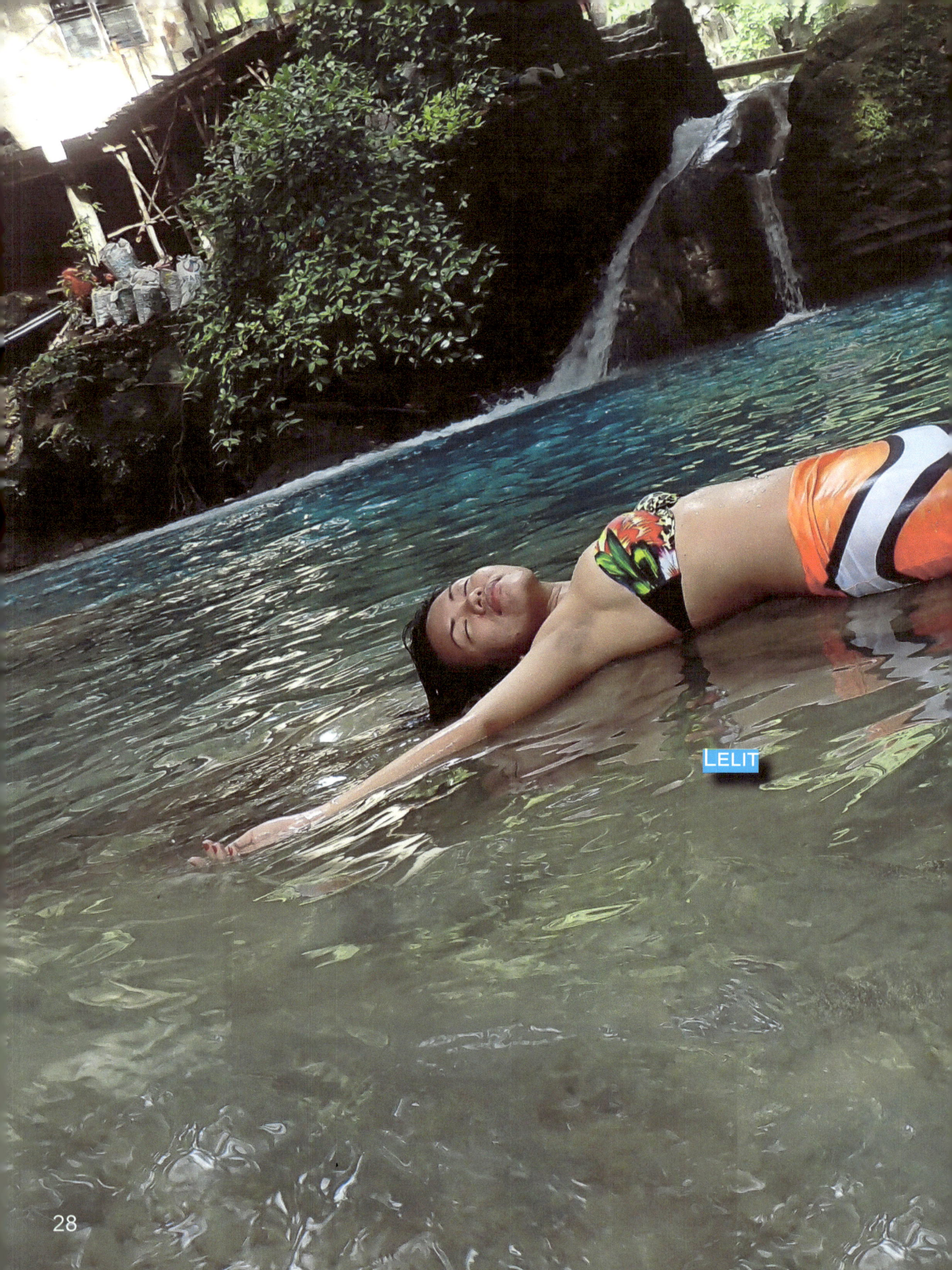

LELIT

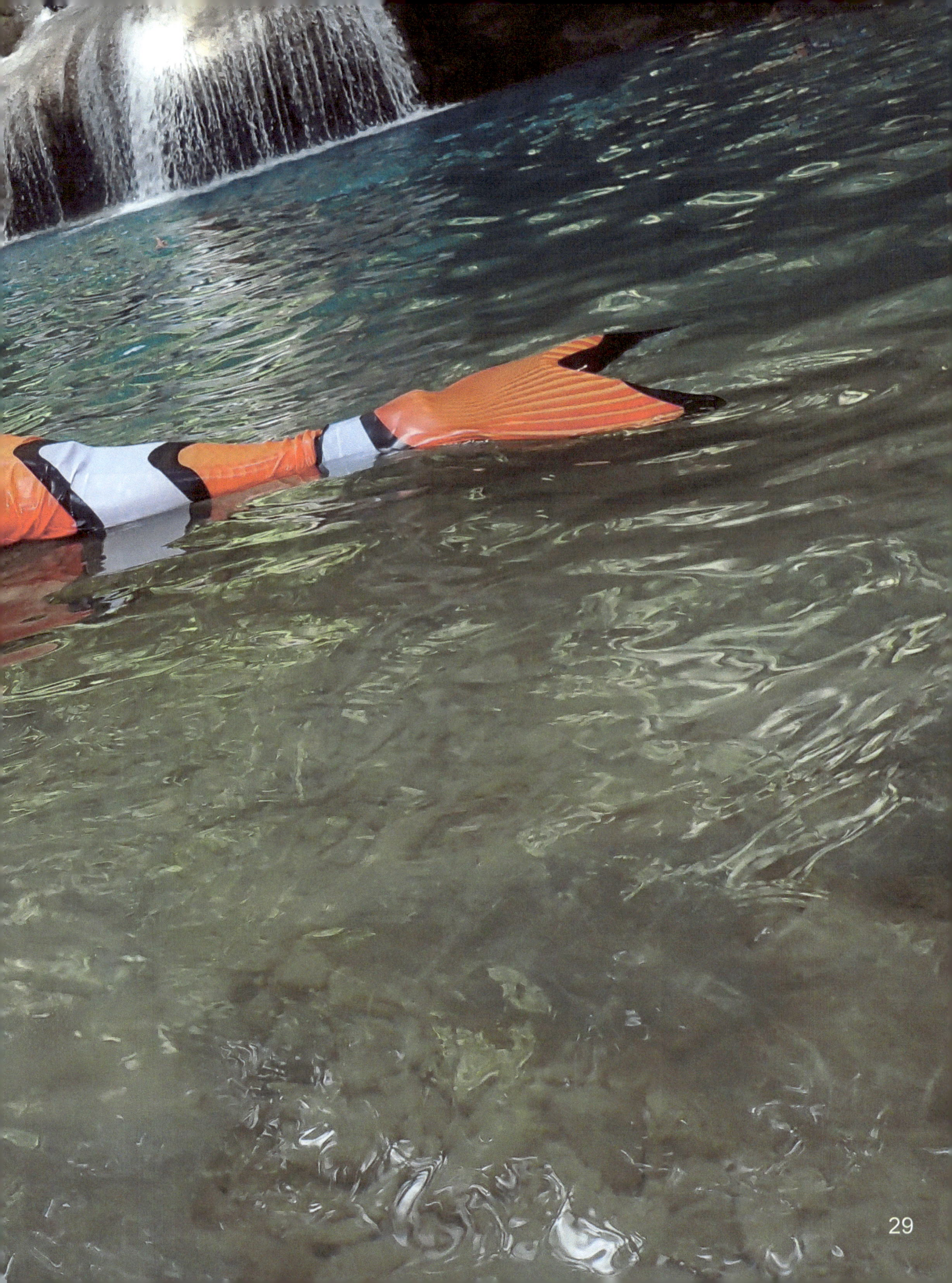

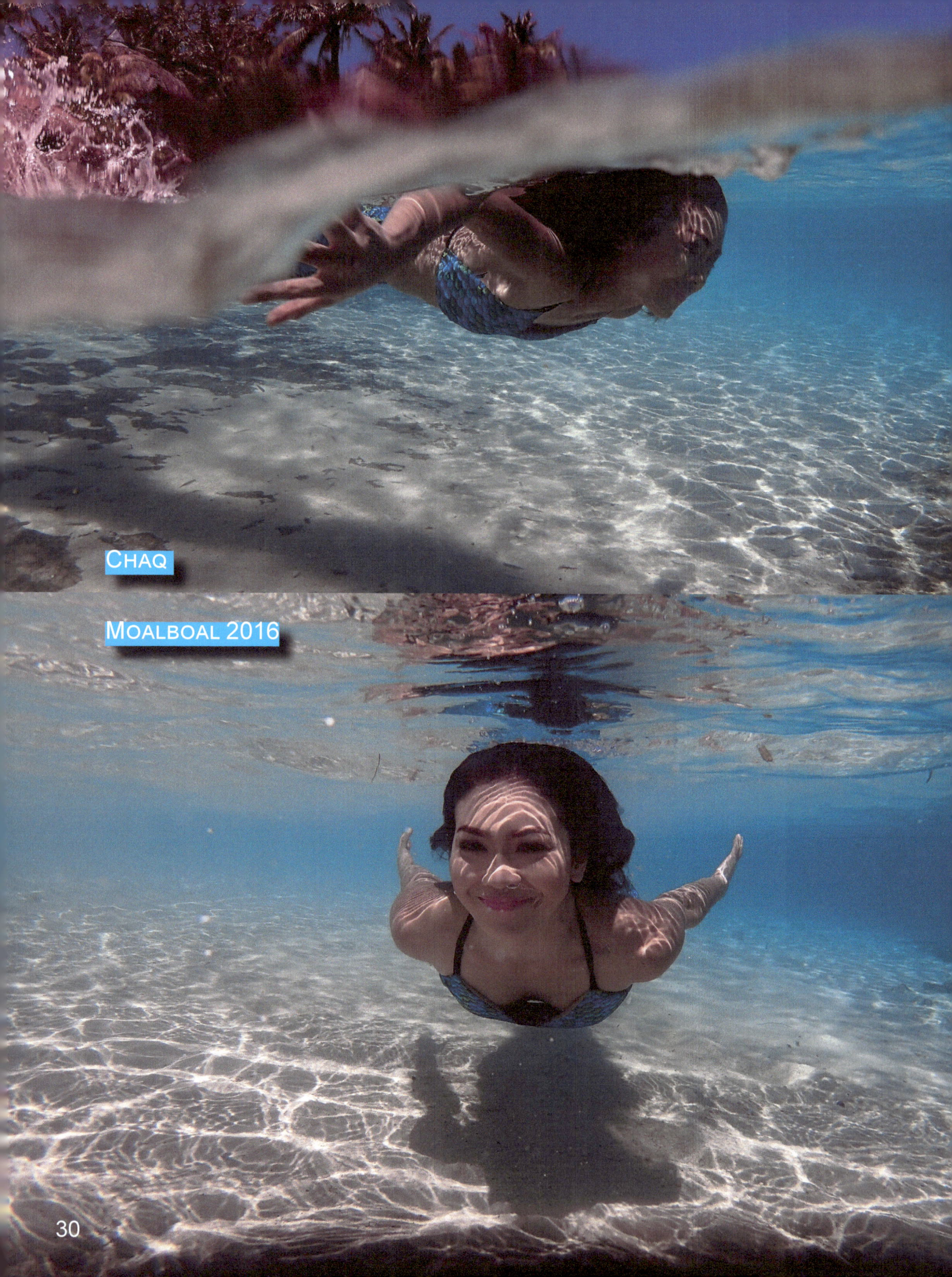

CHAQ

MOALBOAL 2016

30

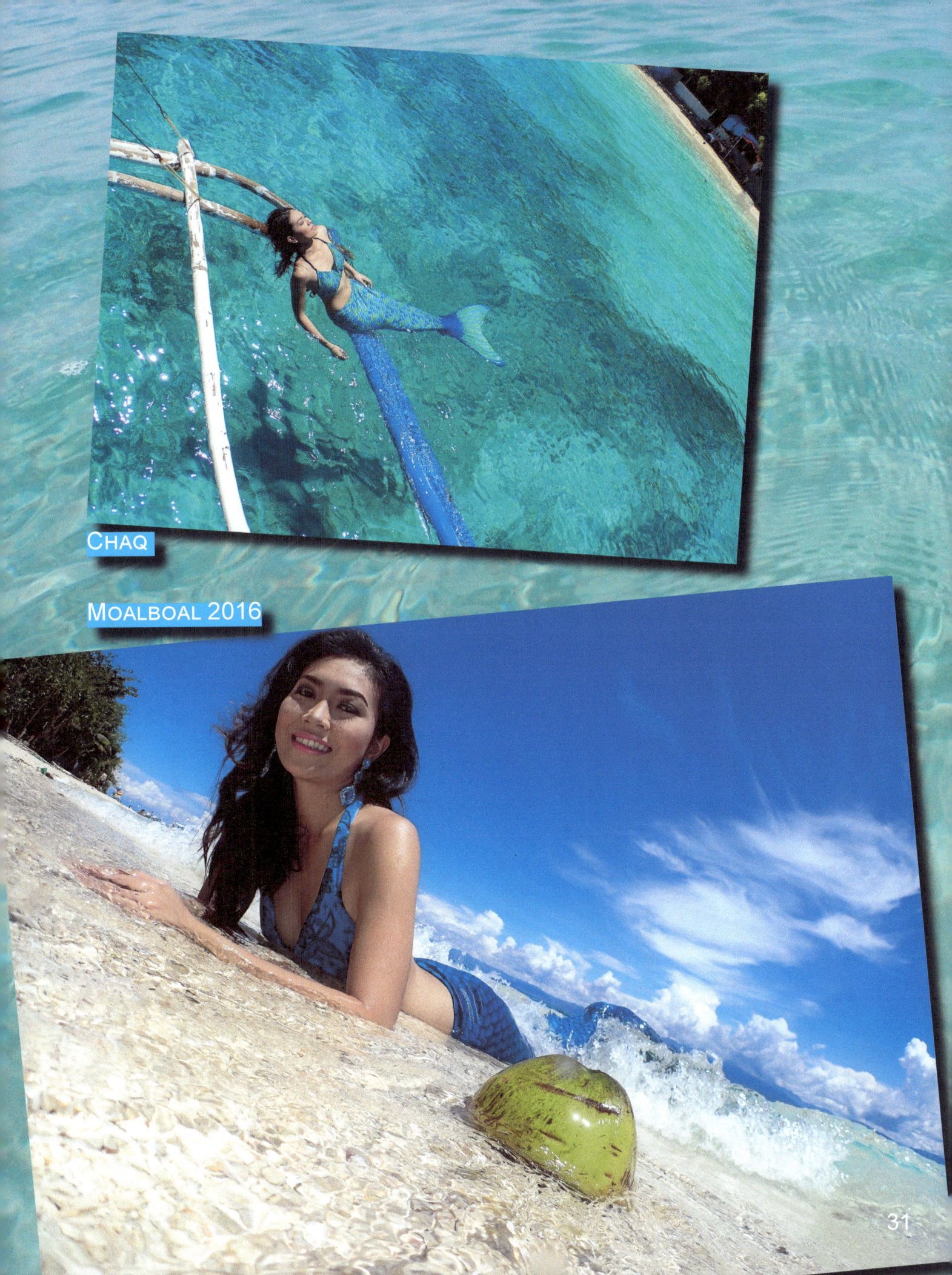

CHAQ

MOALBOAL 2016

31

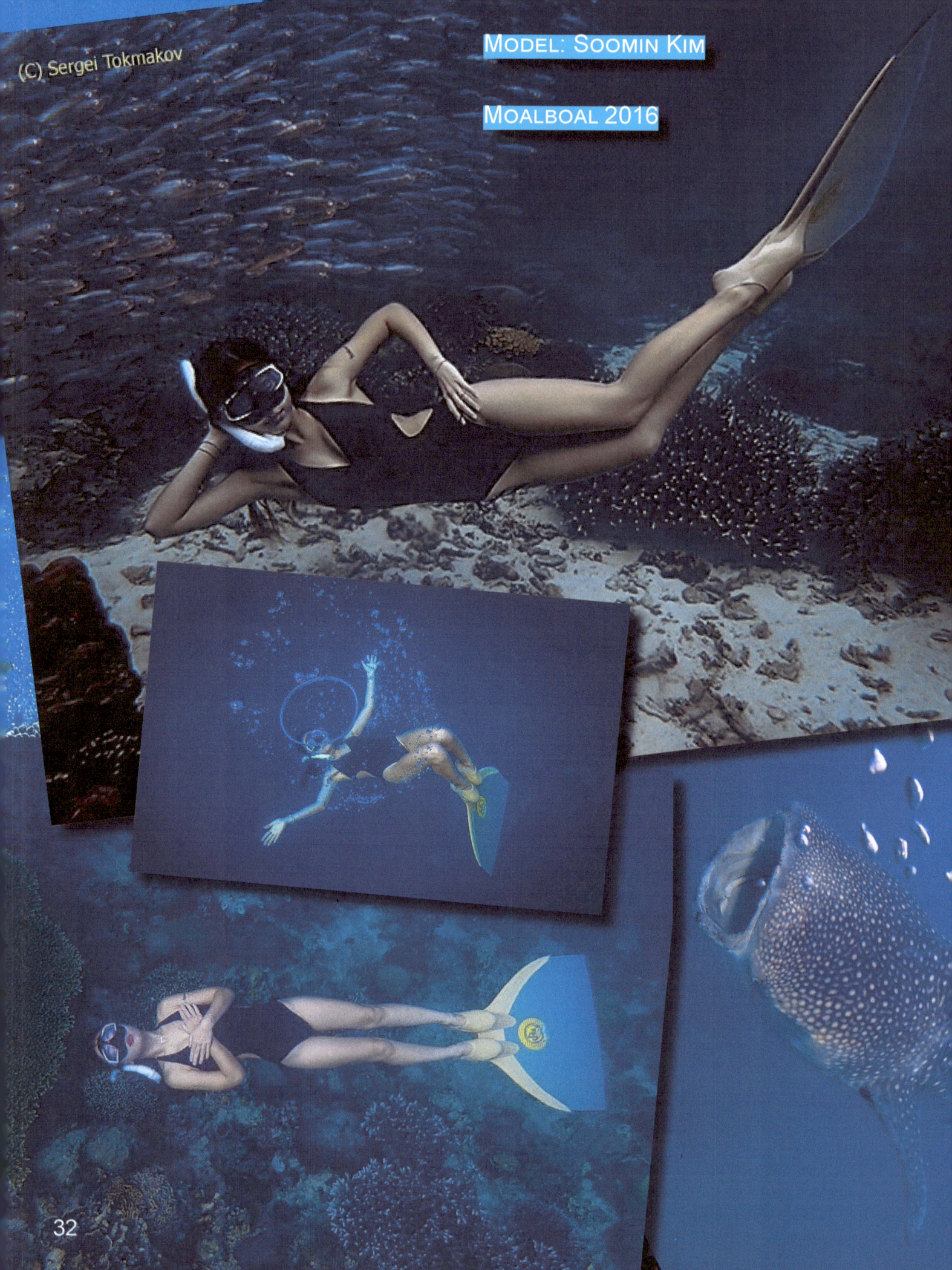

MODEL: SOOMIN KIM

MOALBOAL 2016

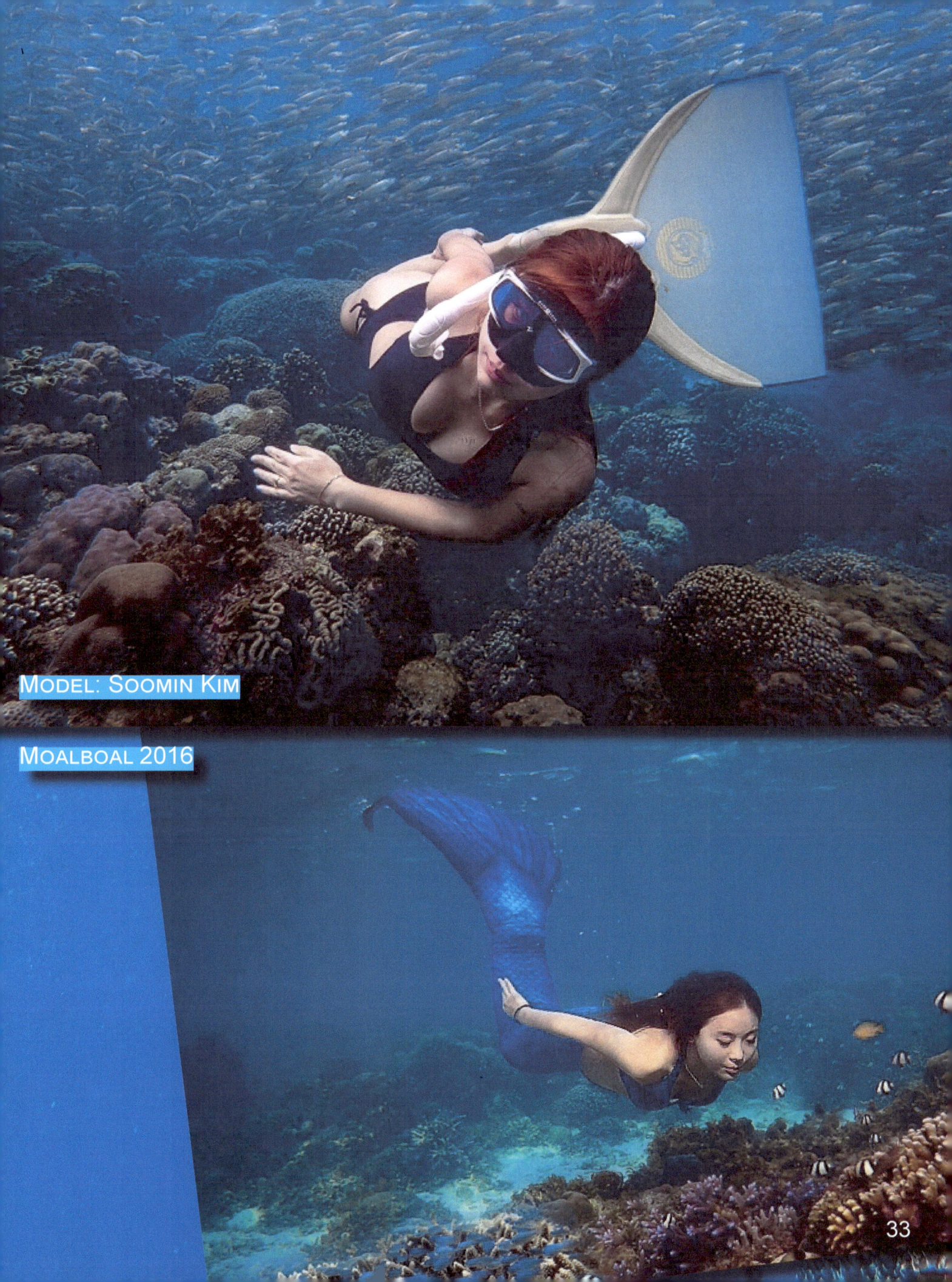

MODEL: SOOMIN KIM

MOALBOAL 2016

33

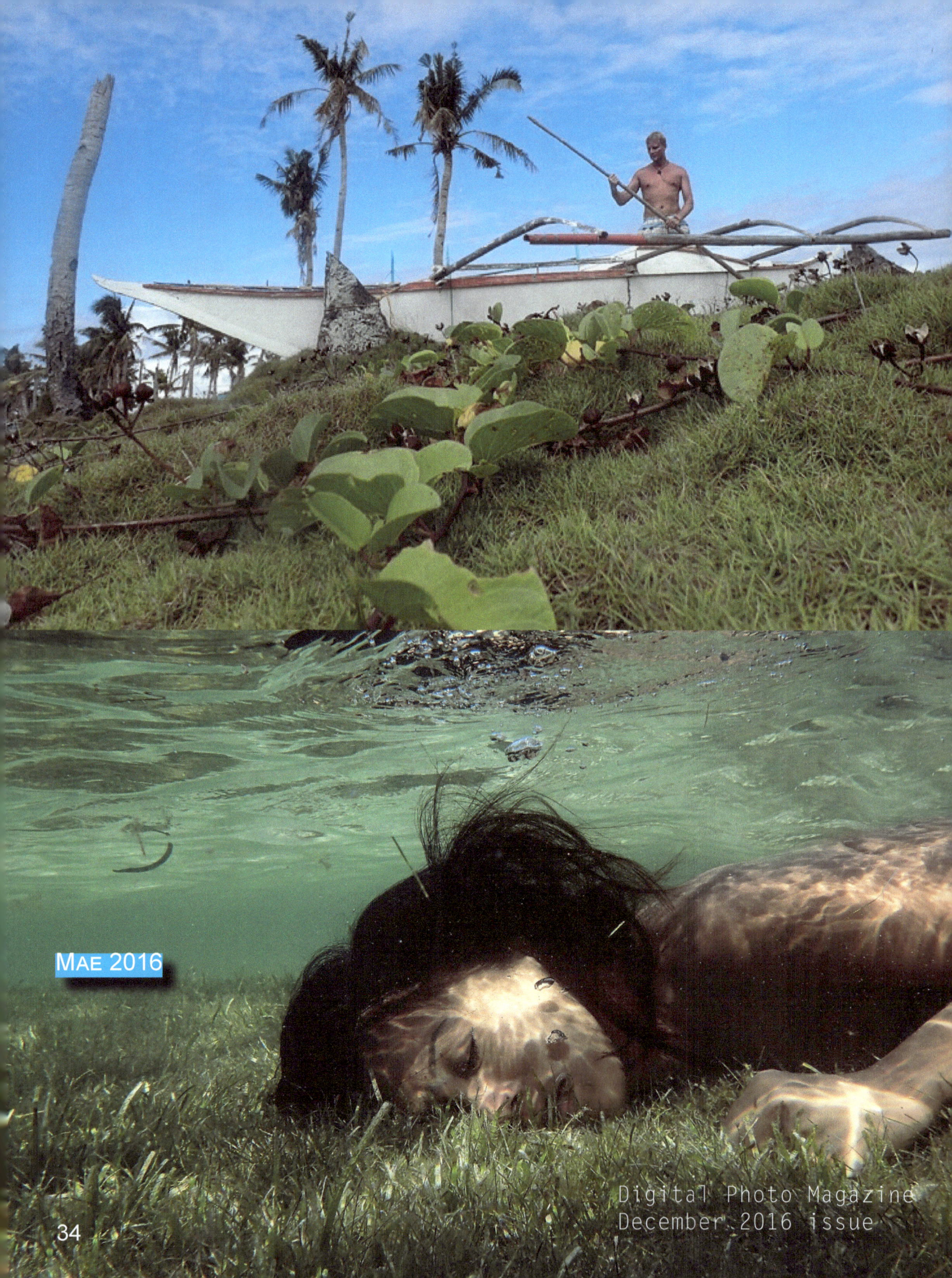

MAE 2016

Digital Photo Magazine
December 2016 issue

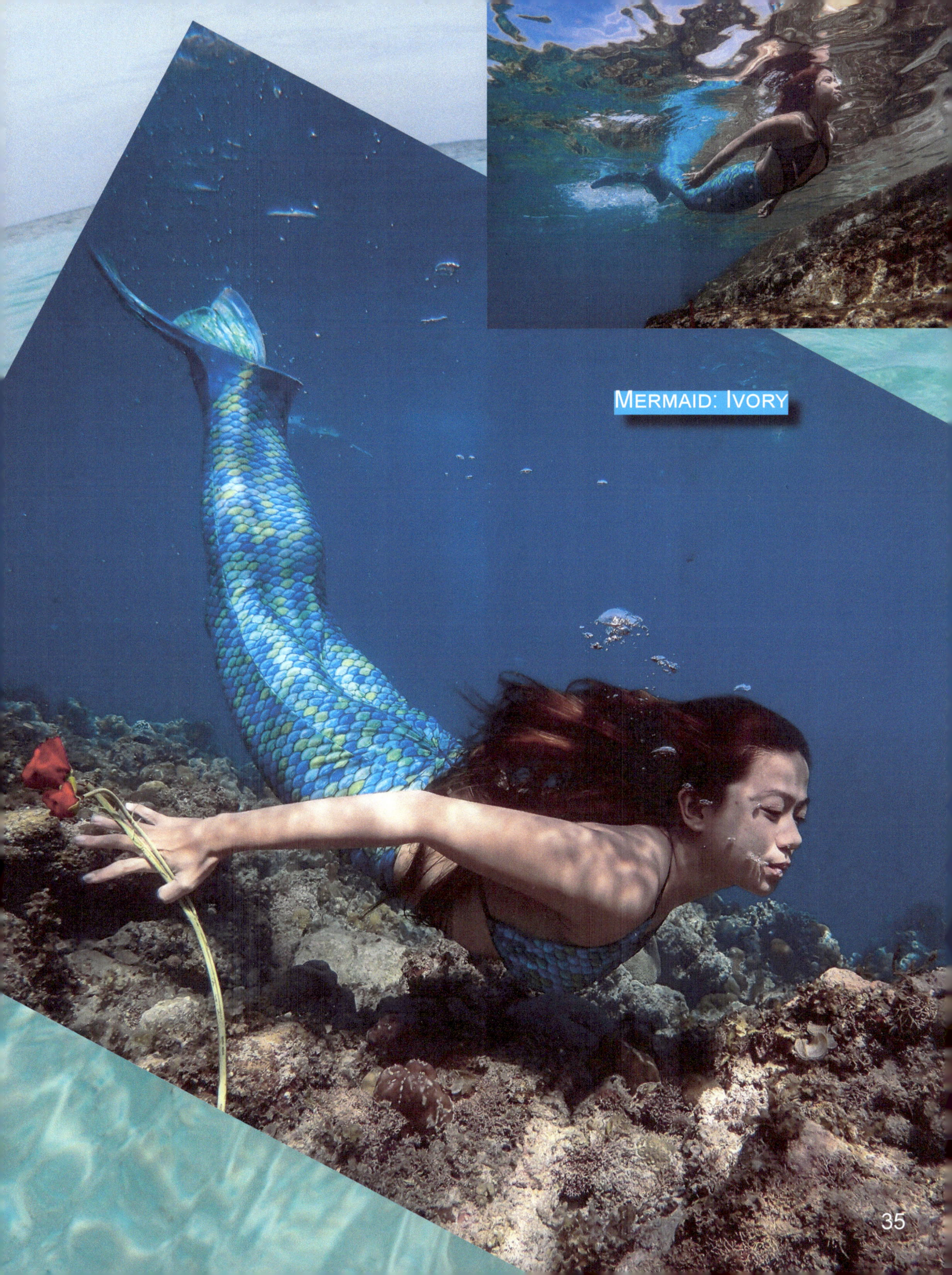

MERMAID: IVORY

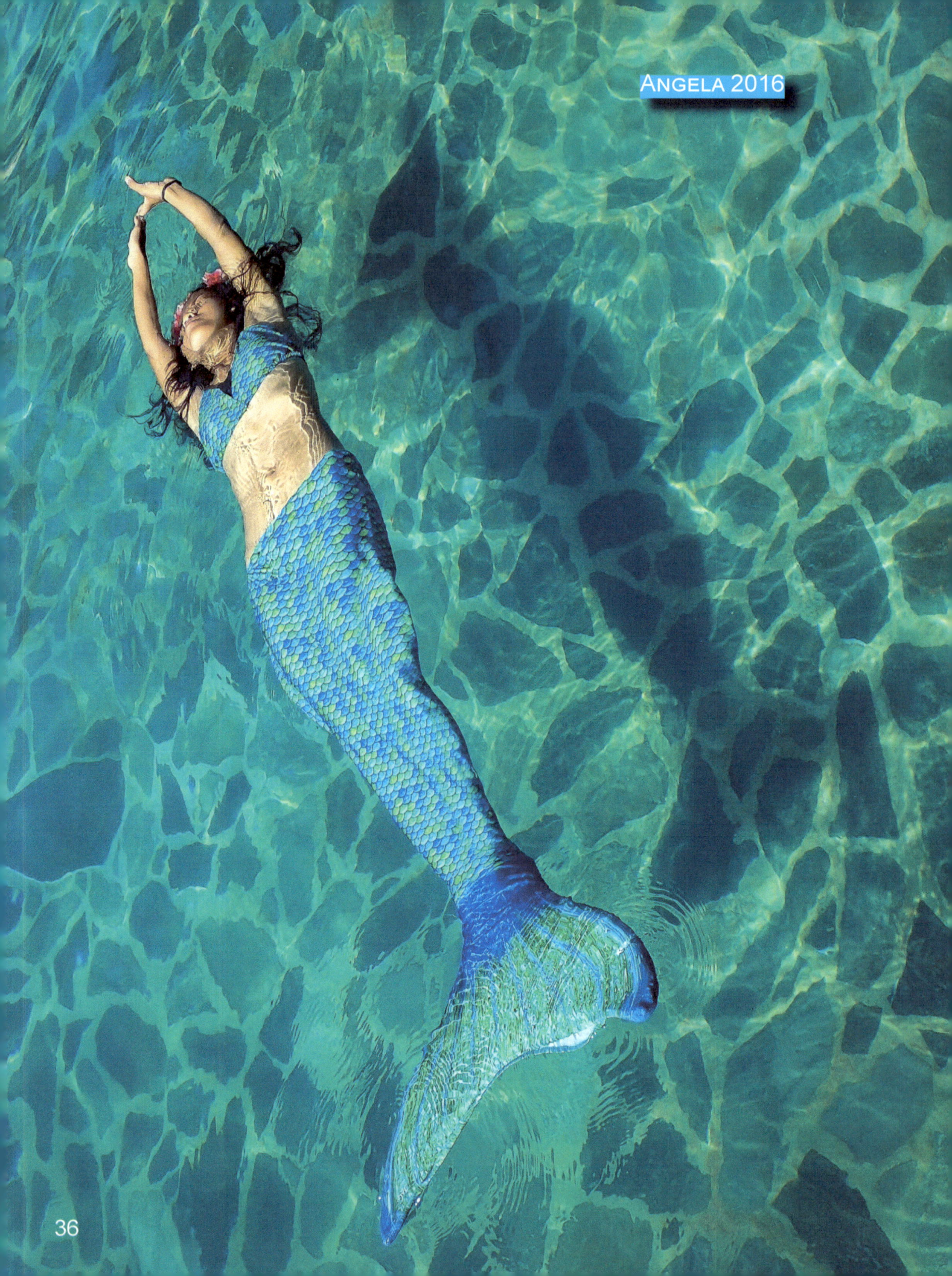

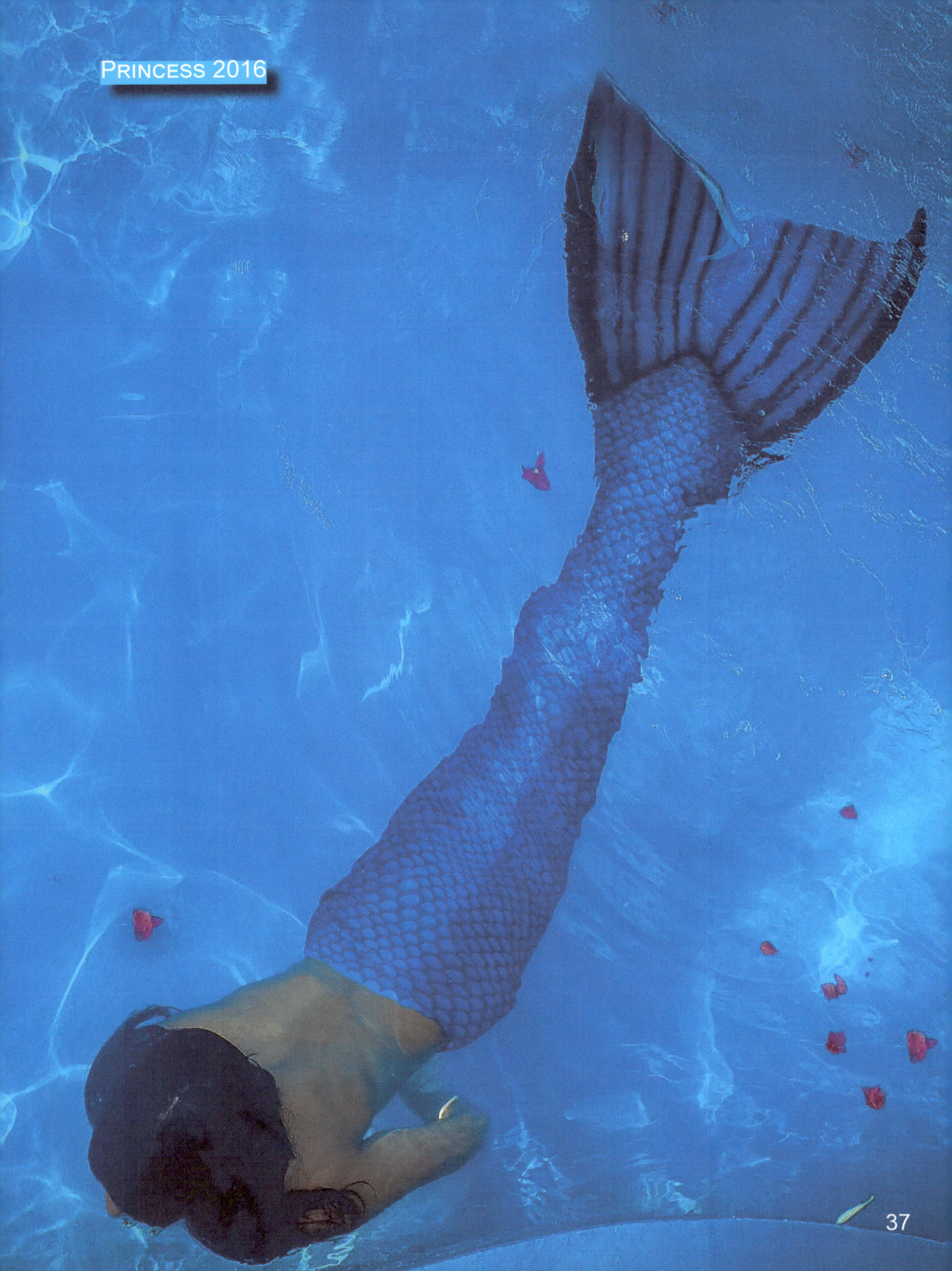

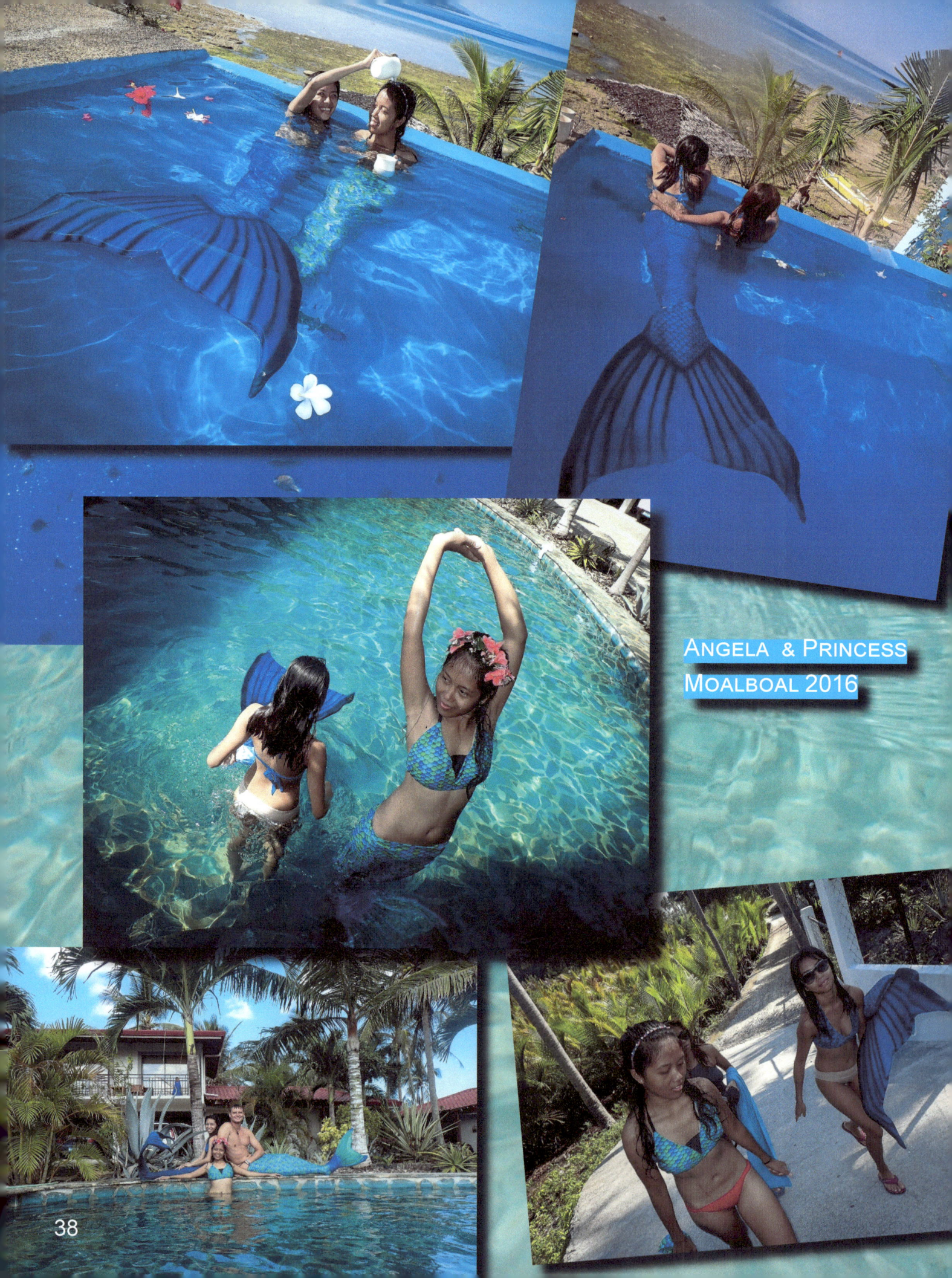

ANGELA & PRINCESS
MOALBOAL 2016

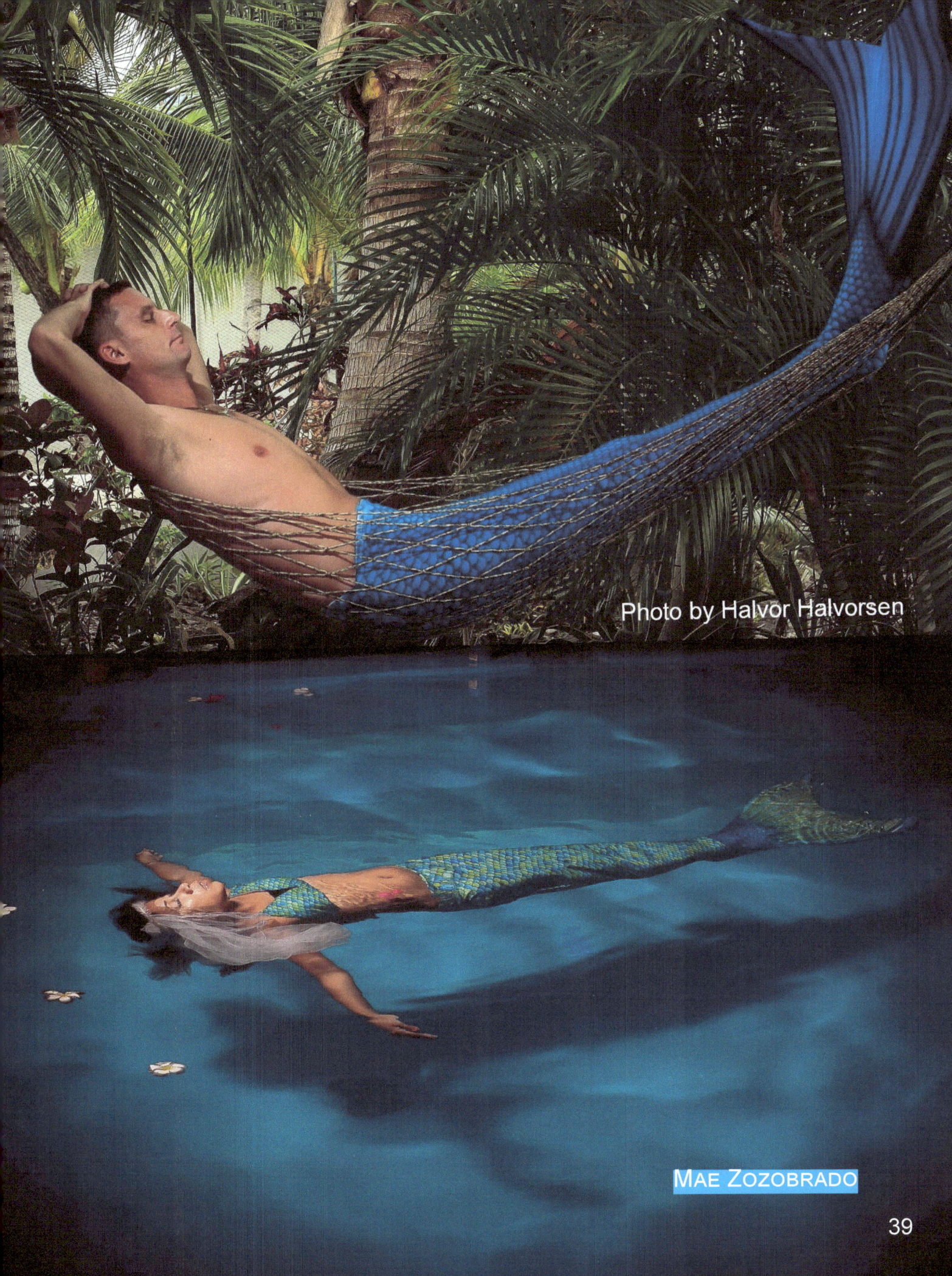

Photo by Halvor Halvorsen

MAE ZOZOBRADO

39

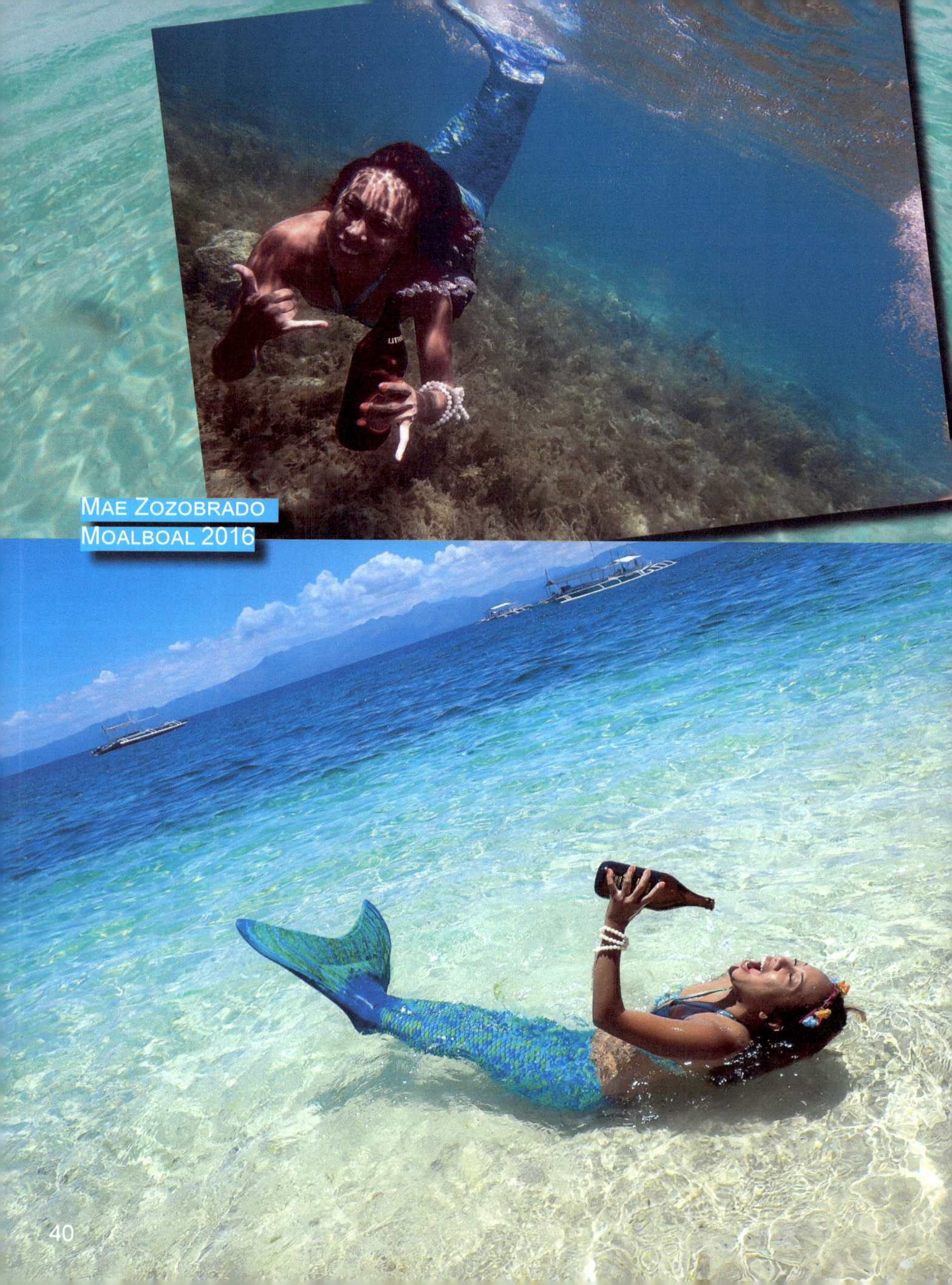

MAE ZOZOBRADO
MOALBOAL 2016

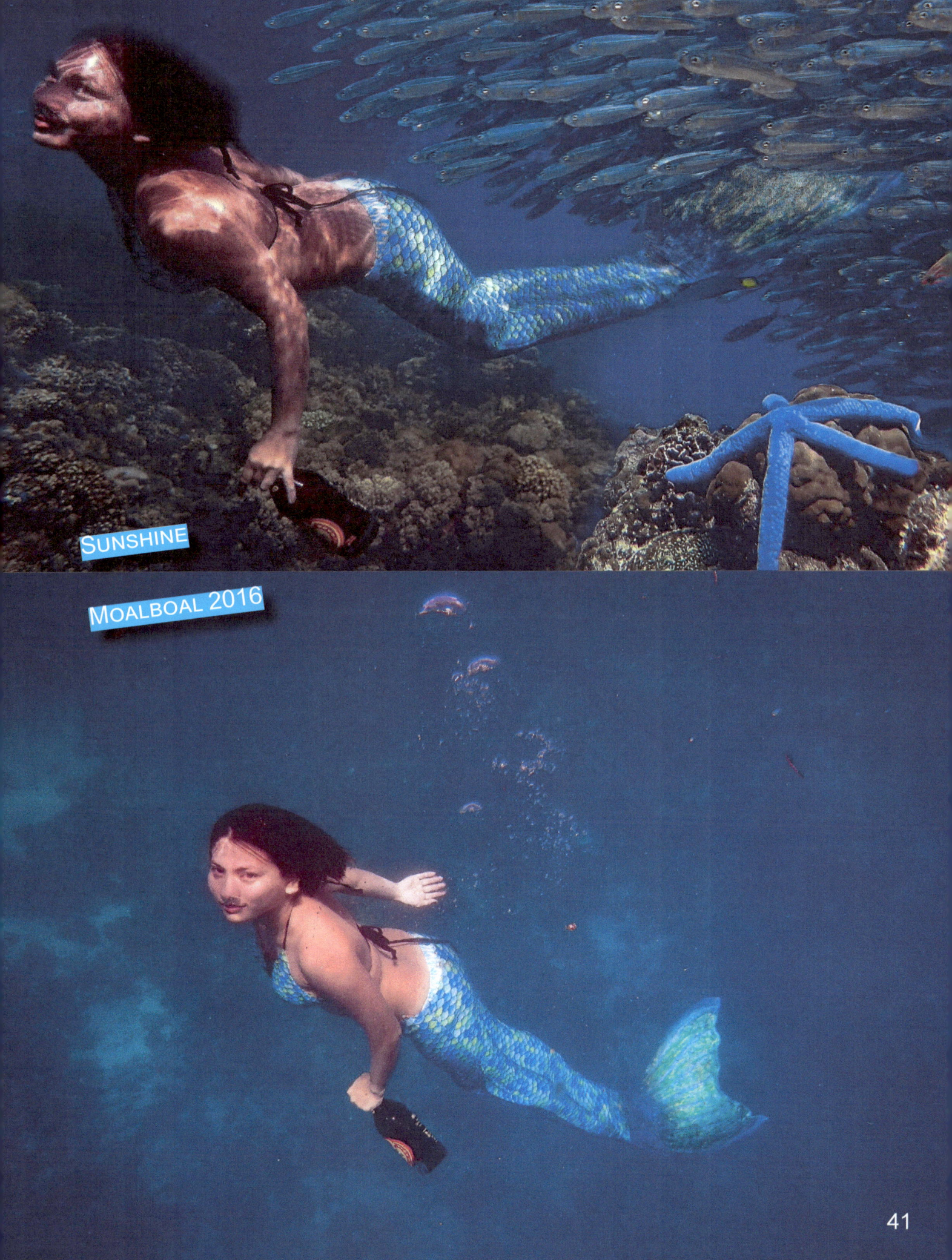

SUNSHINE

MOALBOAL 2016

41

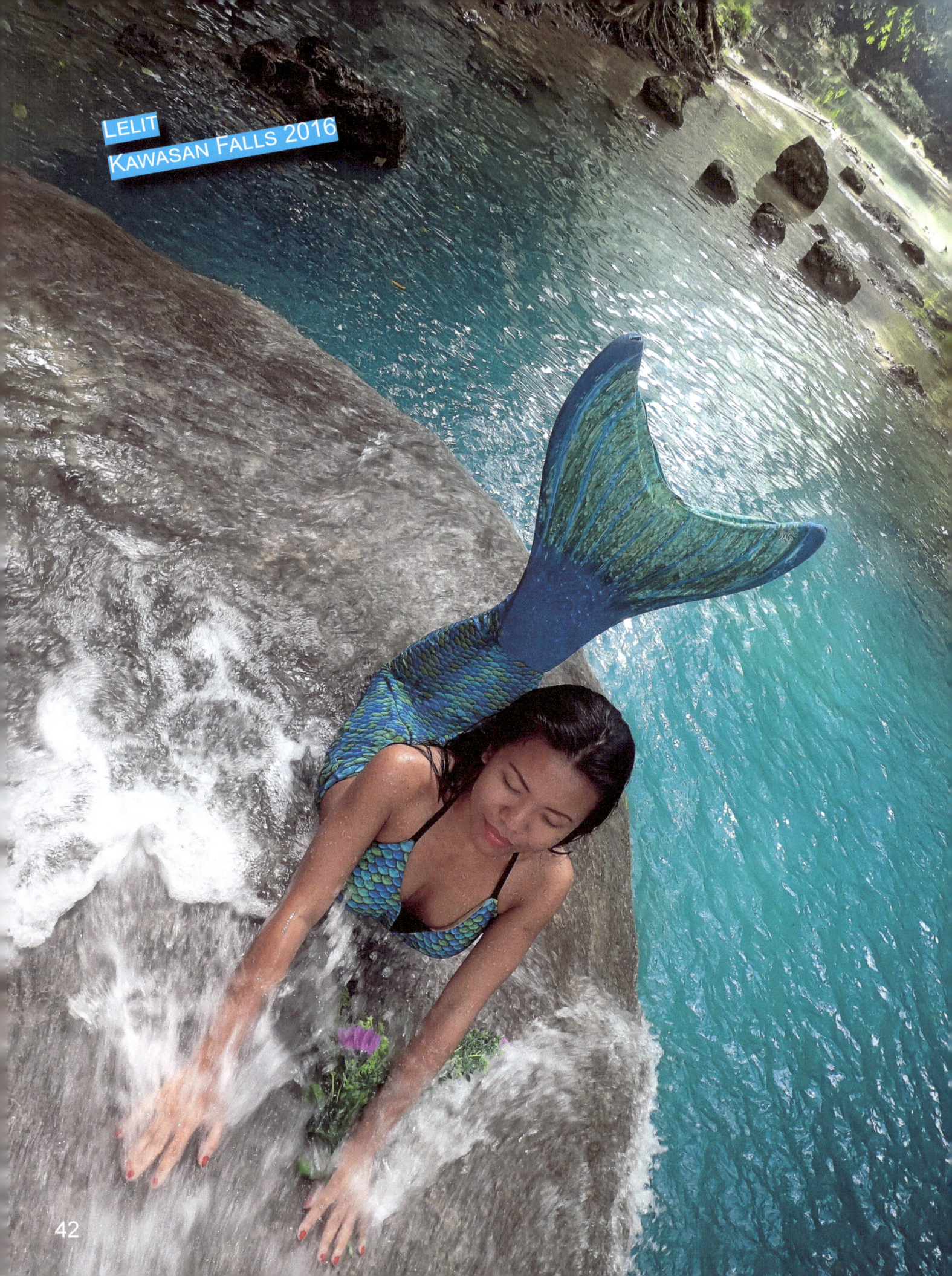

LELIT
KAWASAN FALLS 2016

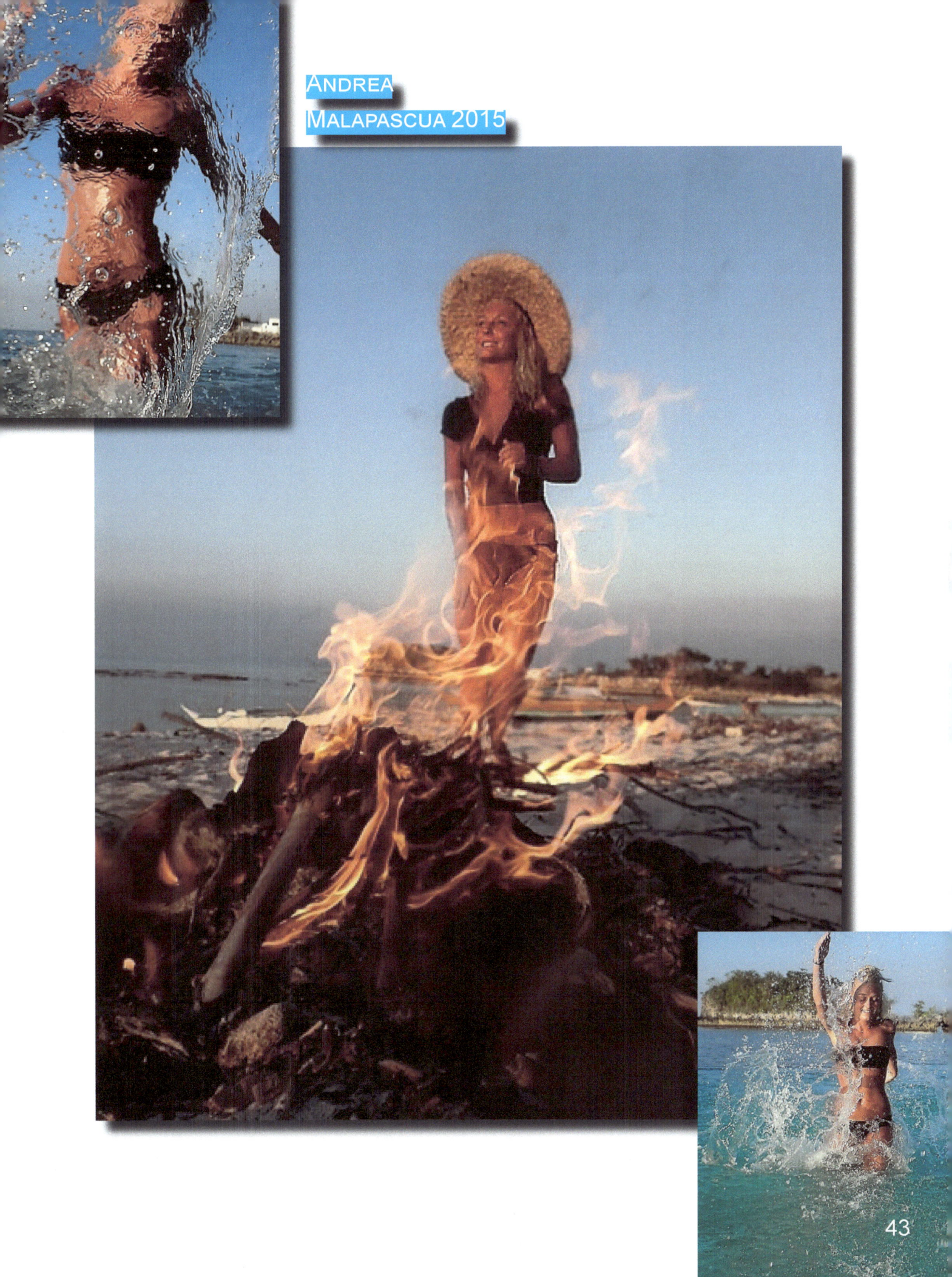

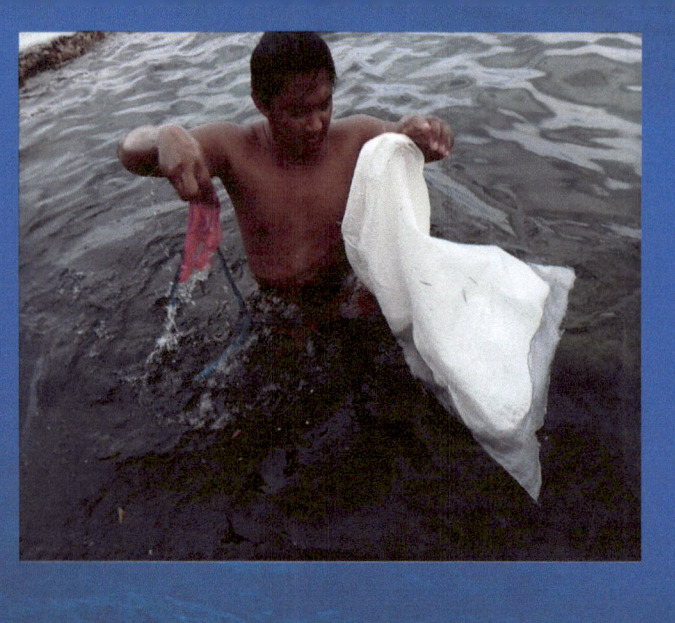

Underwater Beach Cleanup

PANAGSAMA , MOALBOAL
2016

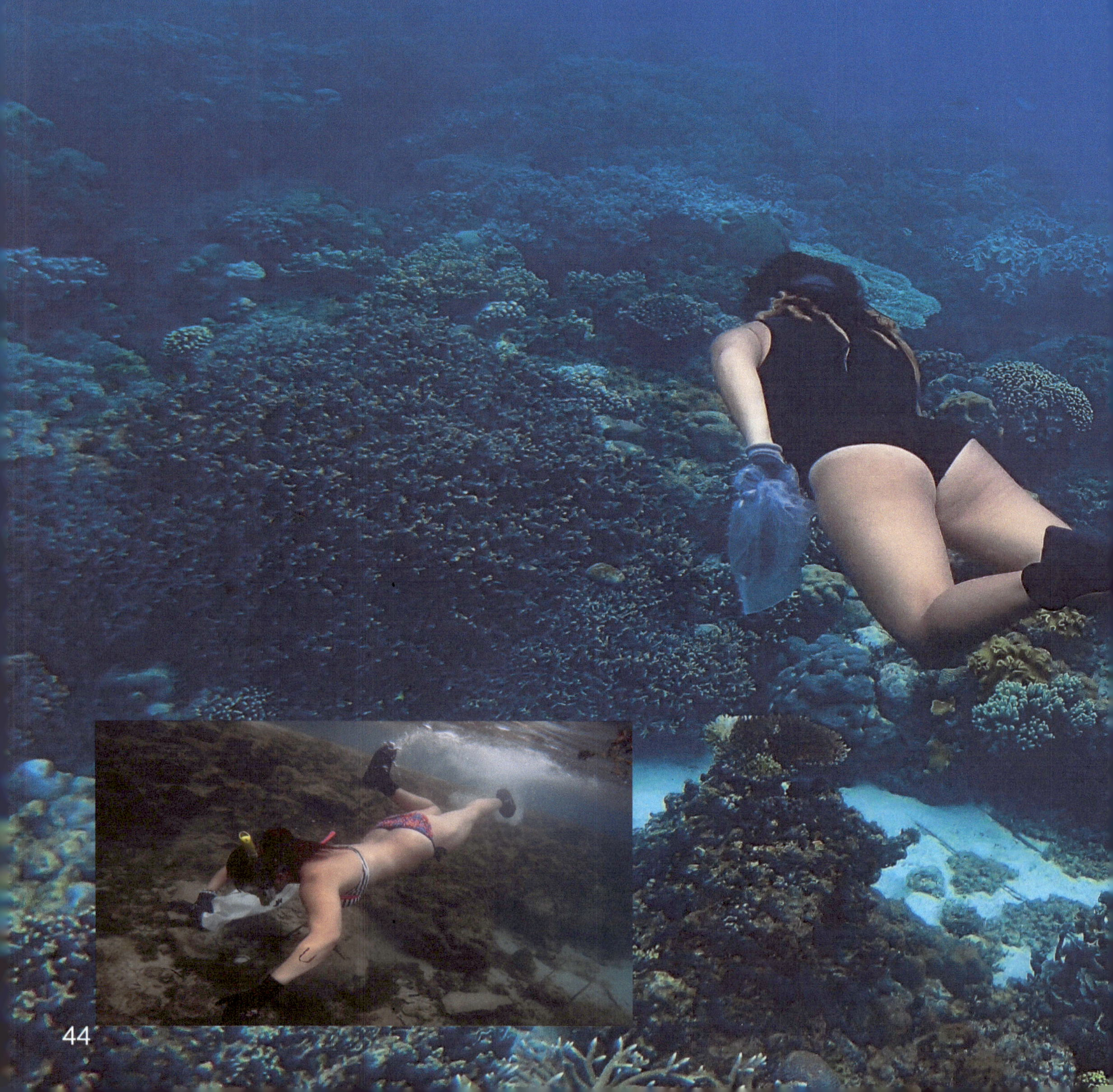

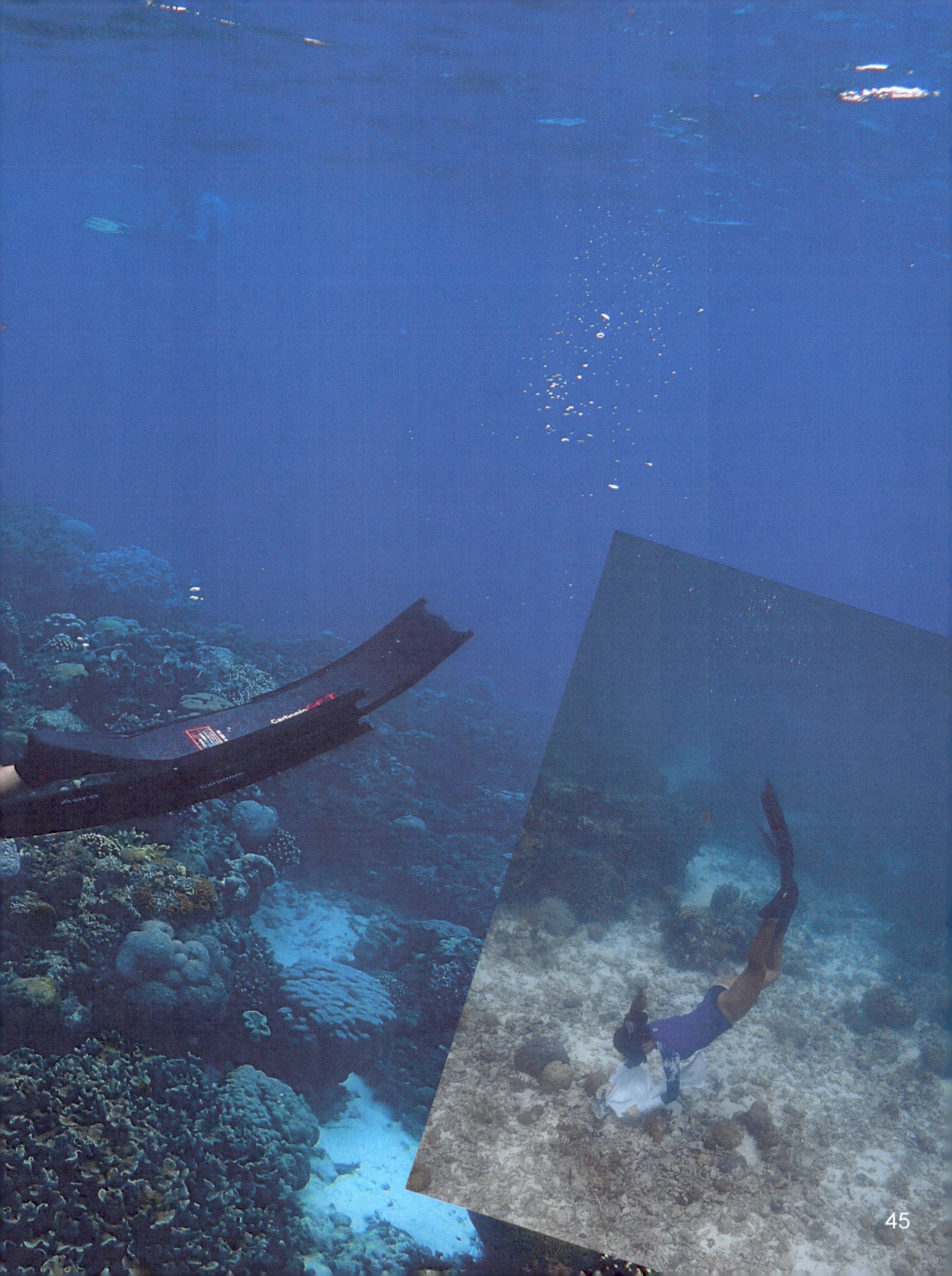

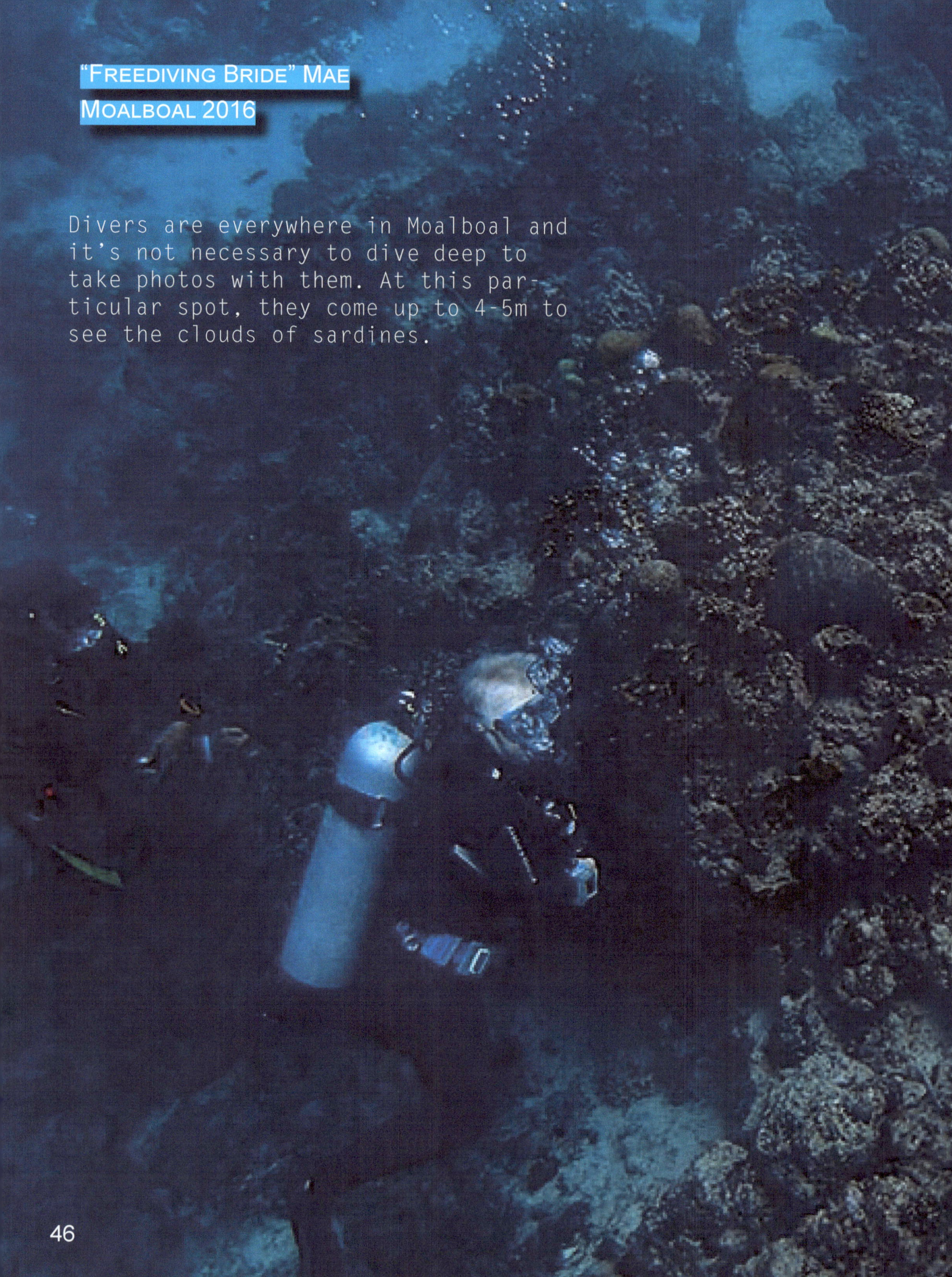

"FREEDIVING BRIDE" MAE
MOALBOAL 2016

Divers are everywhere in Moalboal and it's not necessary to dive deep to take photos with them. At this particular spot, they come up to 4-5m to see the clouds of sardines.

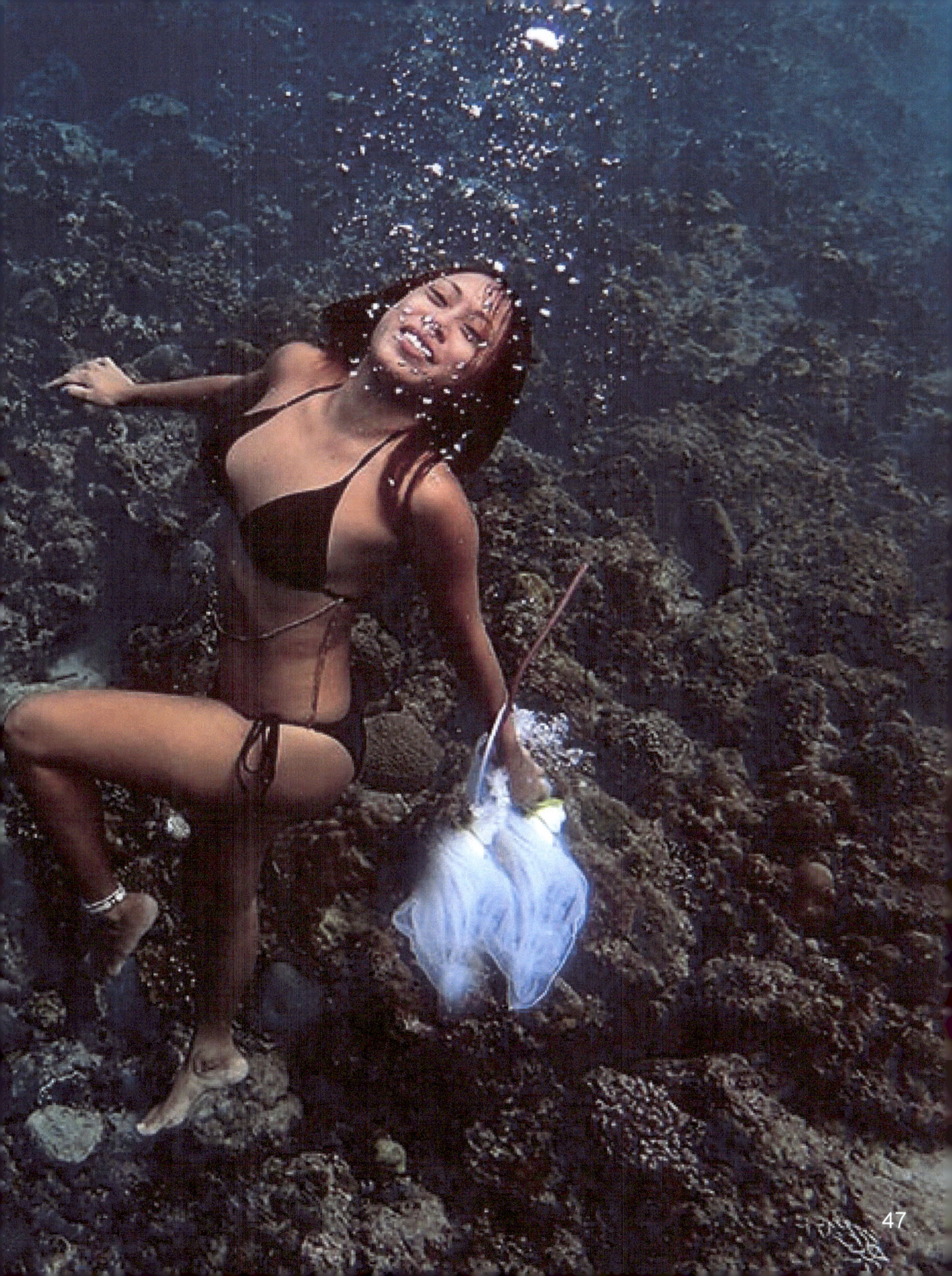

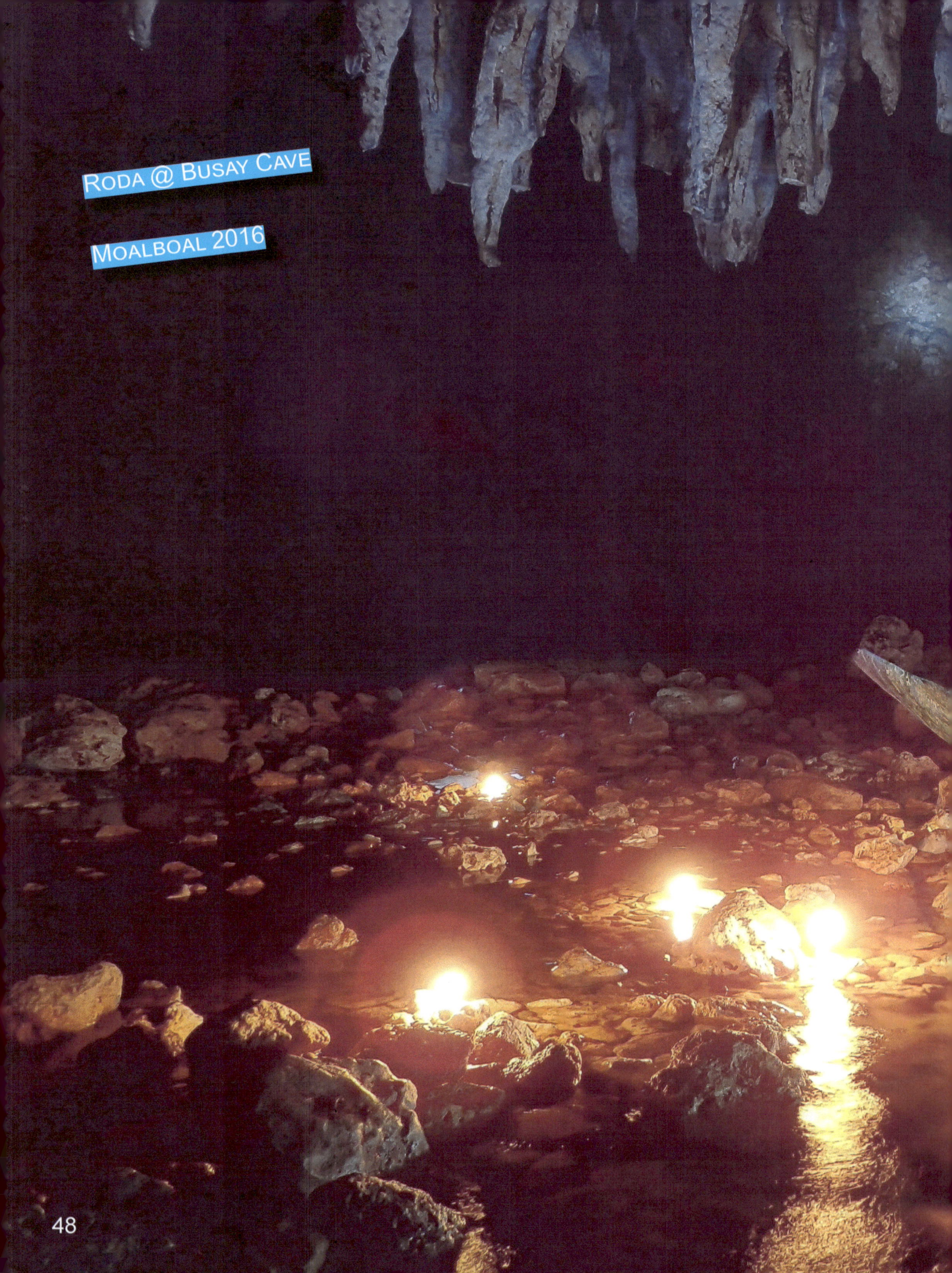

Roda @ Busay Cave

Moalboal 2016

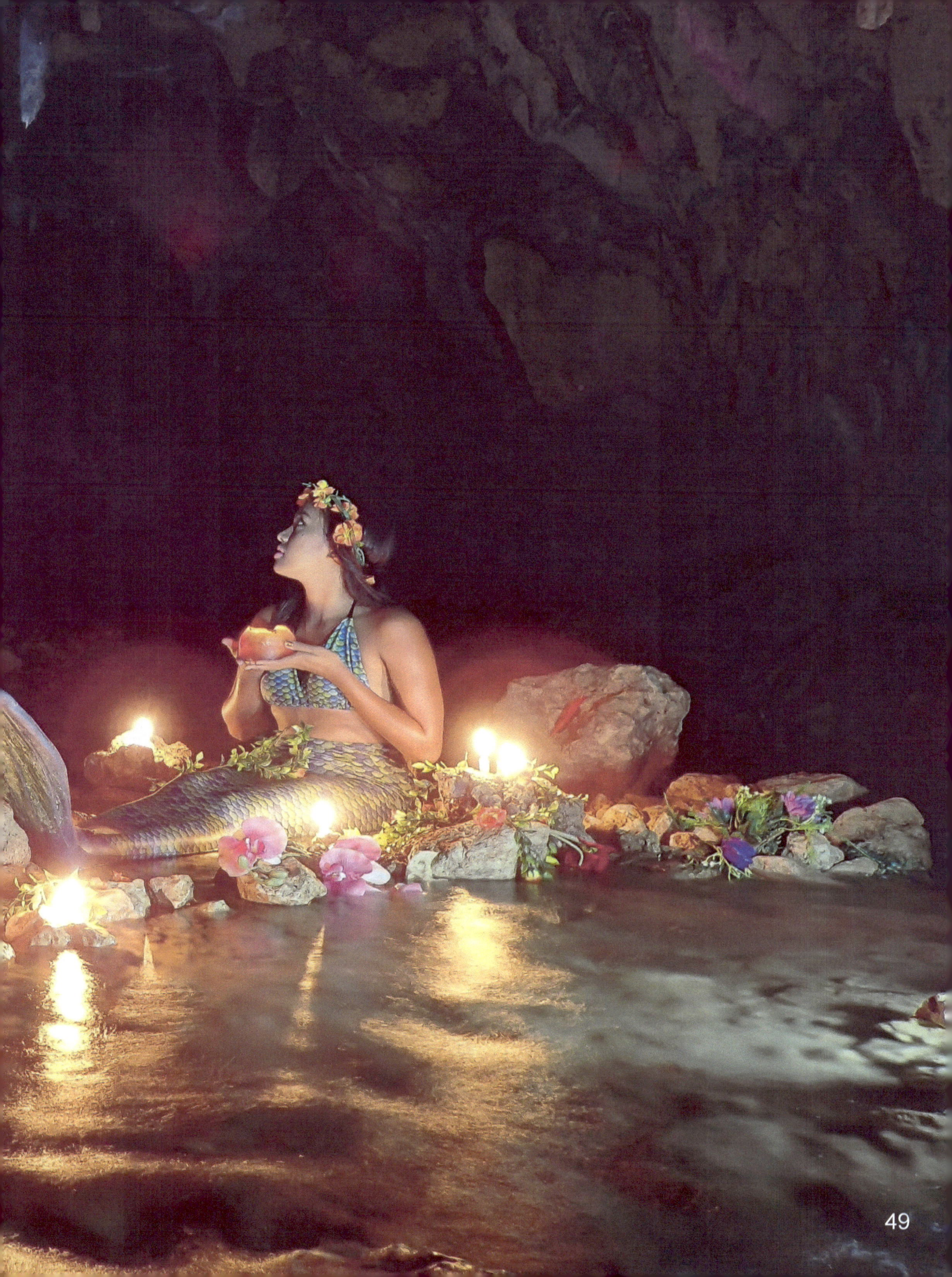

II. WHALE SHARKS

This chapter shows whale sharks that tourists can see in Oslob, Cebu.

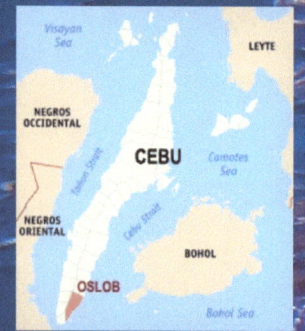

Whale shark watching in Oslob is a controversial tourist attraction. The sharks are fed from boats that bring tourists to swim there. This disrupts the sharks' feeding and migration patterns. The sharks have scars from bumping into those boats. The nutritional value of the food given to them is low. Unfortunately, many tourists do not obey the "no touching" rules.

Proponents of this tourist activity point out to the fact that this attraction is a major source of income for many town residents. Here, they do not slaugher those animals like they do in other countries. The activity is regulated and there is a marine biologist monitoring it.

I am including the whale sharks in the book because it's a wonder of the world that needs to be seen and, hopefully, this will help bring attention to their issues. Everybody is free to make up their own minds.

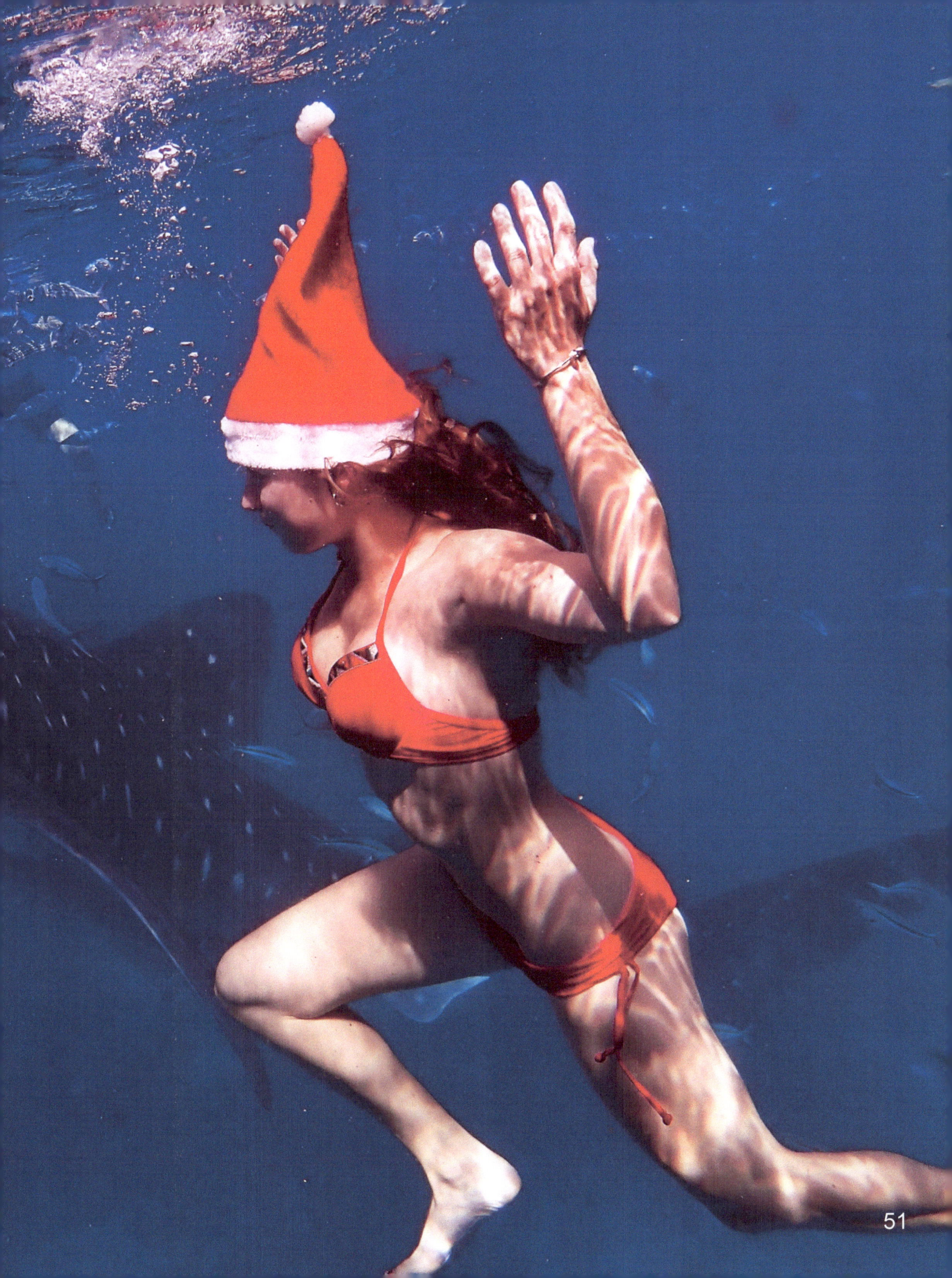

Miss Universe Philippines 2016 Maxine Medina swims with the whale sharks of Oslob. Thanks to the Cebu Provincial Police Office, I had a unique opportunity to photograph the Miss Universe candidates with the whale sharks in December 2016. Photos got published by CNN Philippines, Cosmo Philippines, other (inter)national outlets and, naturally, controversy ensued.

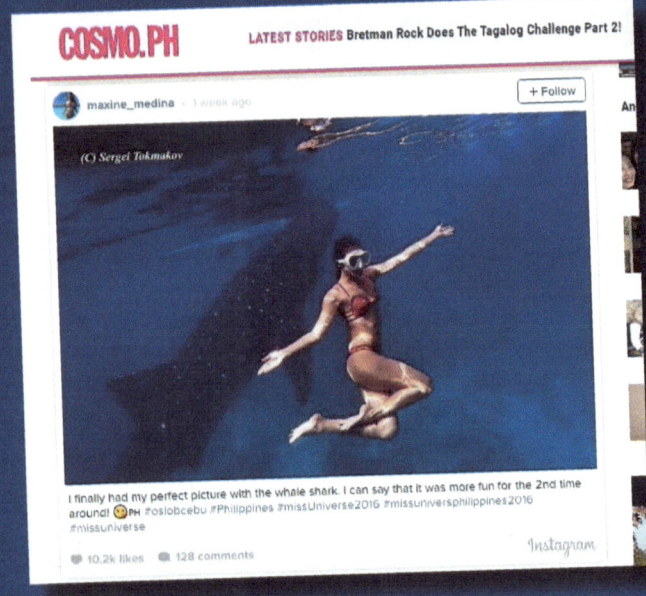

AKTIBIDAD NG MISS UNIVERSE SA OSLOB, BINATIKOS

CNN Philippines

HEADLINES · RUSSIAN ENVOY: SYRIA HAS RETAKEN EASTERN ALEPPO · BALITAAN

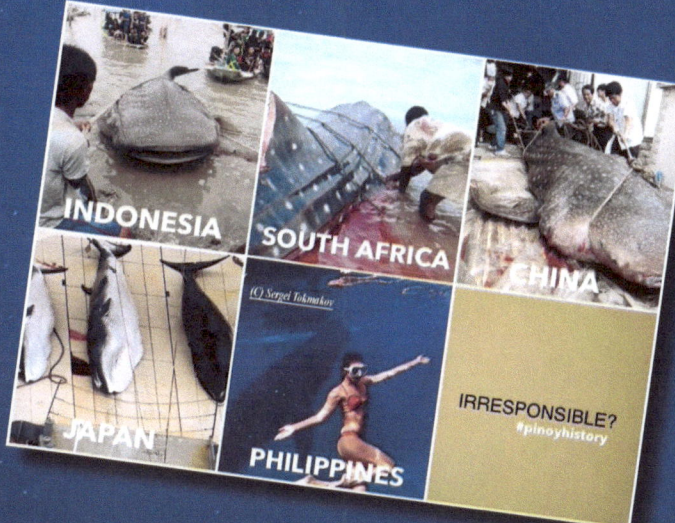

INDONESIA · SOUTH AFRICA · CHINA

JAPAN · (C) Sergei Tokmakov · PHILIPPINES · IRRESPONSIBLE? #pinoyhistory

> *"While environmentalists have some very valid points, let's not forget that the whale shark watching program feeds the whole town of Oslob. Animals are important but thousands of struggling humans are more so.*
>
> *In many countries, they slaughter whale sharks just so that a handful of people can profit. In Oslob, people carefully feed and swim with them, for the benefit of the whole community."*

Attorney Sergei Tokmakov

TRENDING NOW

DOT DEFENDS WHALE SWIMMING OF MISS U CANDIDATES

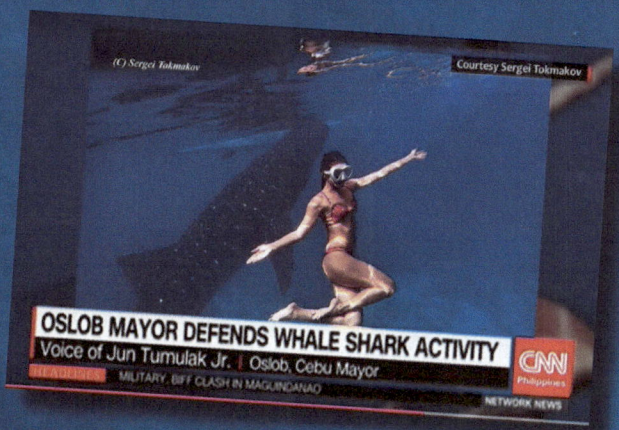

(C) Sergei Tokmakov · Courtesy Sergei Tokmakov

OSLOB MAYOR DEFENDS WHALE SHARK ACTIVITY

Voice of Jun Tumulak Jr. | Oslob, Cebu Mayor

CNN Philippines

HEADLINES · MILITARY, BIFF CLASH IN MAGUINDANAO · NETWORK NEWS

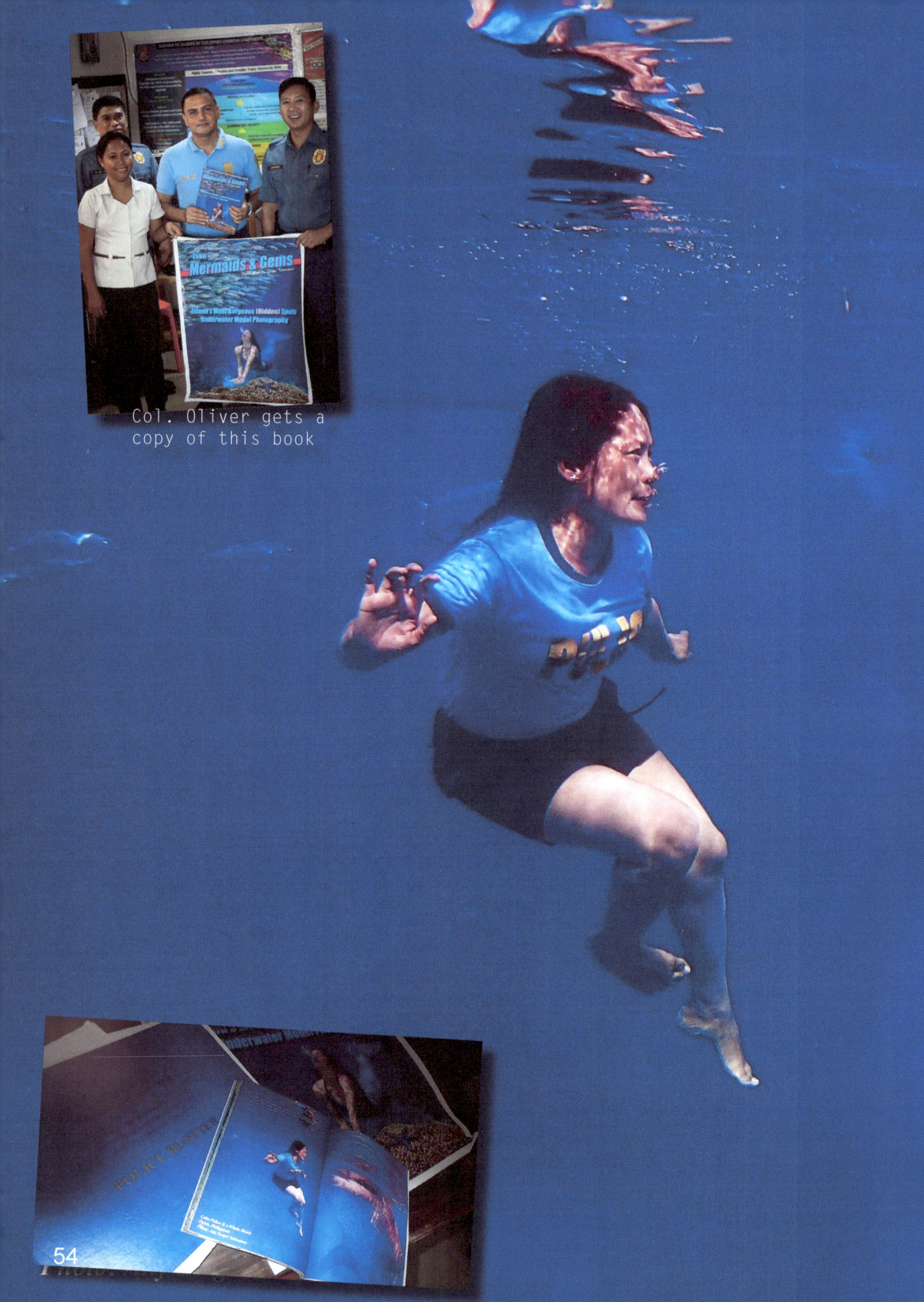

Col. Oliver gets a
copy of this book

Cebu's top cops organized this photo shoot for the resulting posters to go into the tourist police offices throughout the island:
-    Director of the Cebu Provincial Police Office, Col. Eric Noble
-    Chief of Cebu Prov. Tourist Police, Col. Richard Oliver

Here is how my colorful, fruitful and unusual friendship with the Philippine Natn't Police (PNP) began. I met the aforementioned Colonels when I attended a canyoneering trip that they organized. It was at a time when Western embassies issued a set of travel advisories warning of terrorist plots to kidnap foreigners in the area. Authorities were taking measures to prevent foreigner stampede off the island. The PNP was also trying to improve its image among foreigners due to constant criticism from the Western media on the extrajudicial killings in the drug war. Foreigners were invited to attend the police canyoneering trip but I was the only one who showed up.

Cops were very friendly, like Filipinos always are, and I immediately realized that this can be a win-win partnership. It was good for their image to have an American lawyer take nice pics portraying them as local heroes. It was good for me because the PNP provided me access to some of the most interesting people and photo ops. That's because they were often called on to escort important people to beautiful locations. E.g., Miss Universe candidates & Thai Princess swimming with the whale sharks, Singaporean Ambassador visiting a tiny perfect island, various politicians visiting gorgeous waterfalls, etc. Another big benefit to me was that I got to attend various security conferences where I was usually the only foreigner present, so I could have the most up-to-date information on the security situation on the island.

So, I became a tourist police volunteer, official photographer, and eventually started wearing a uniform. Felt super safe and always had a great time with them while helping the community. It was definitely a win-win.

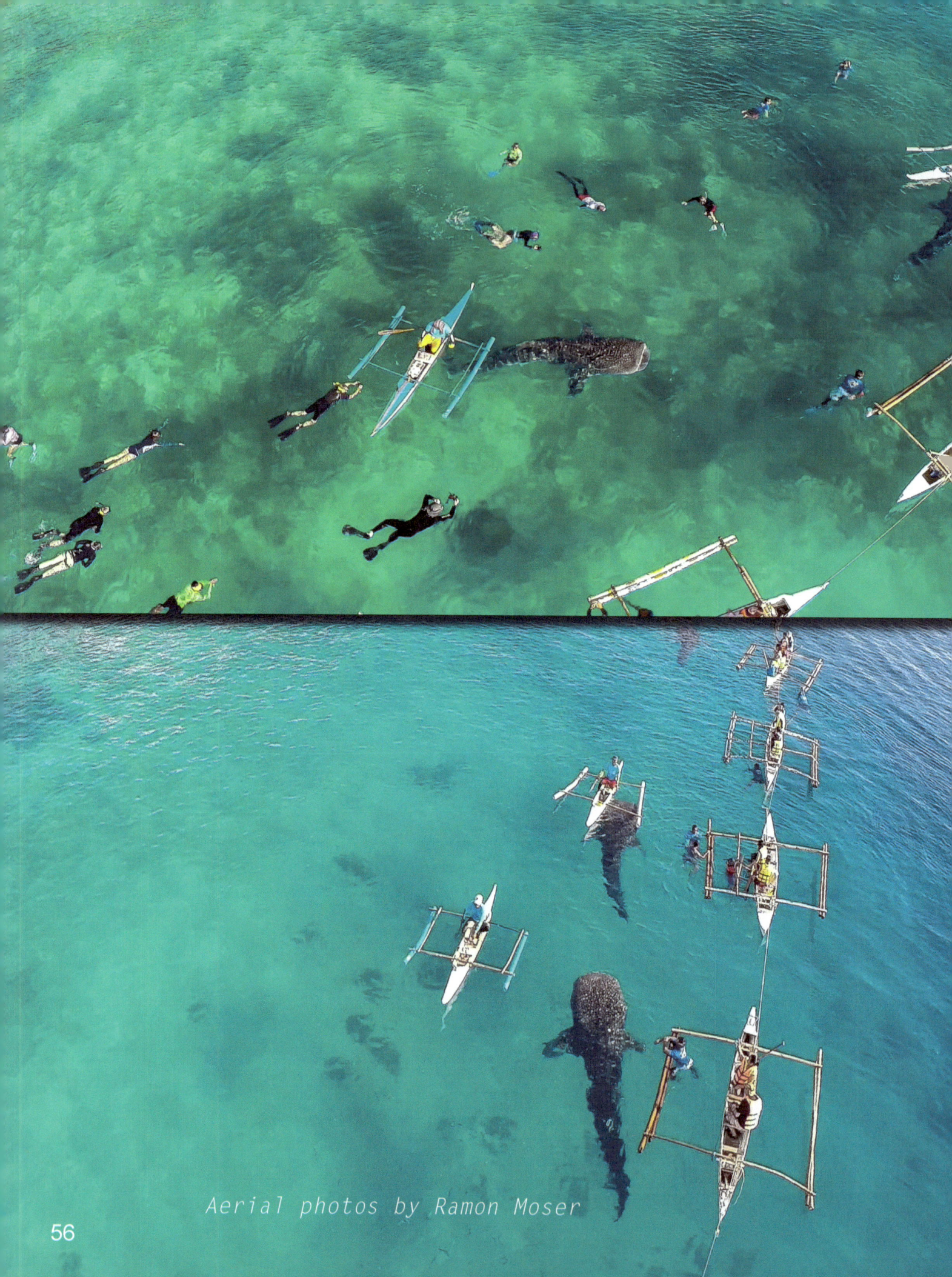

Aerial photos by Ramon Moser

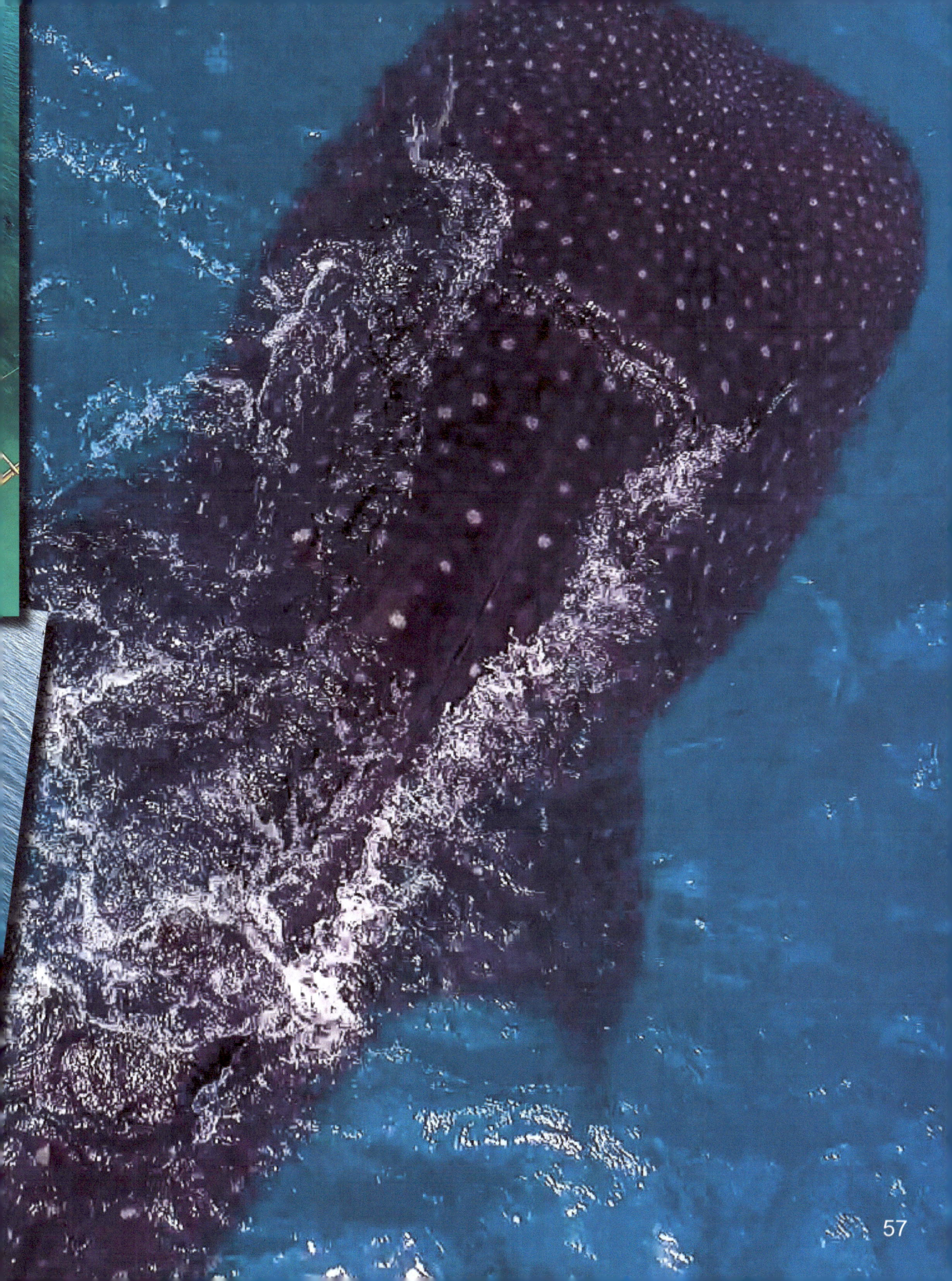

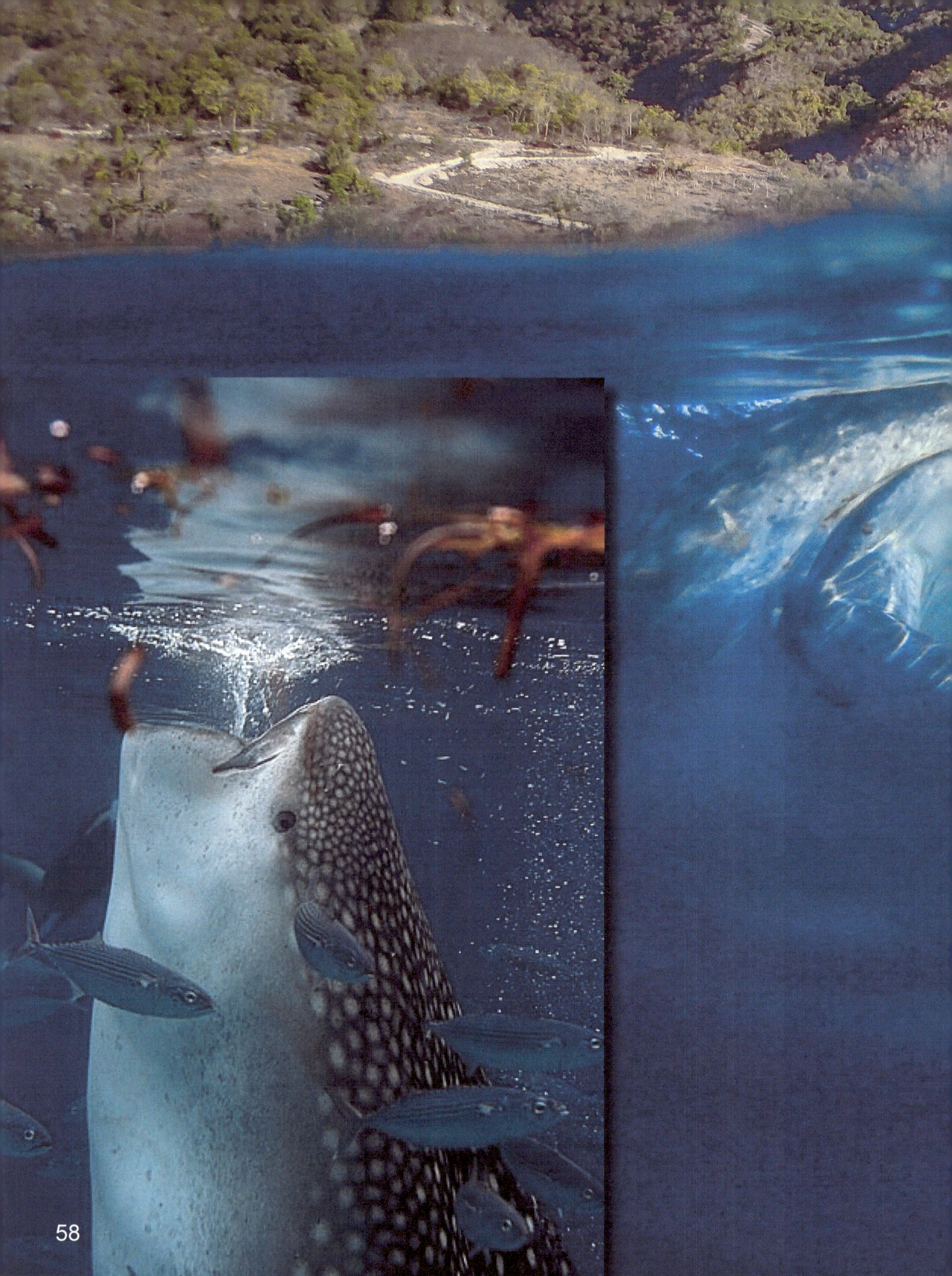

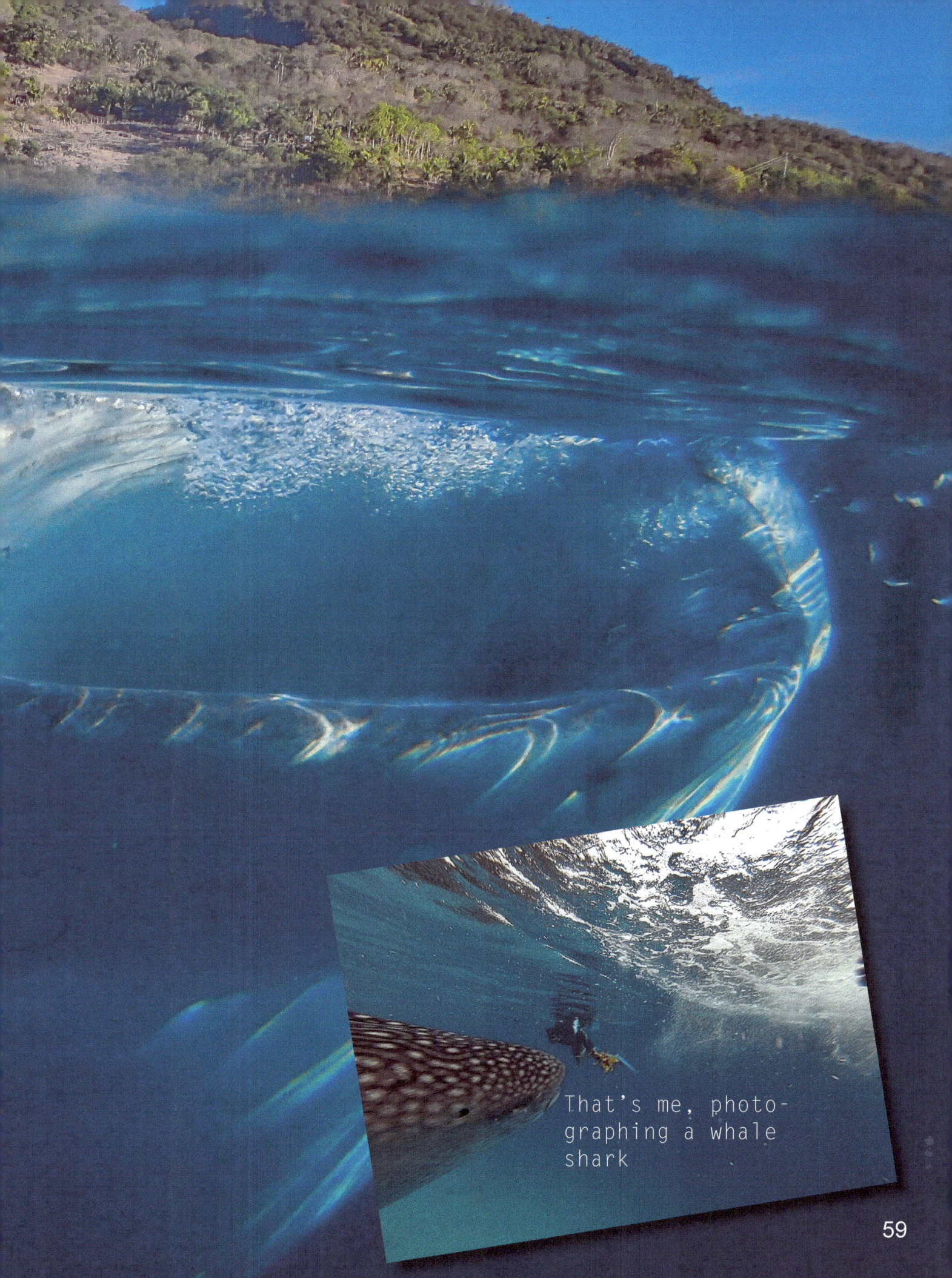

That's me, photographing a whale shark

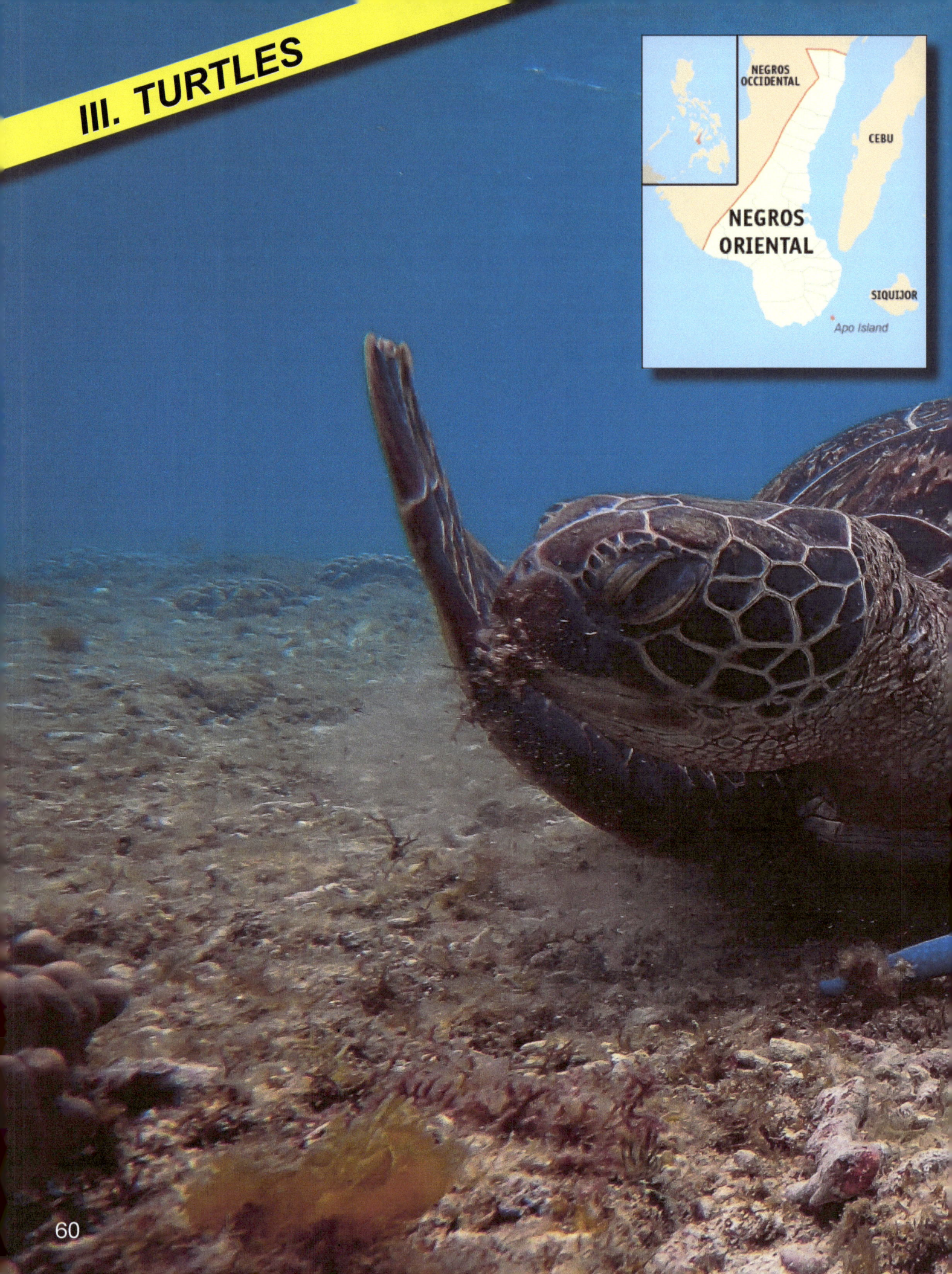

NEGROS
OCCIDENTAL

CEBU

NEGROS
ORIENTAL

SIQUIJOR

Apo Island

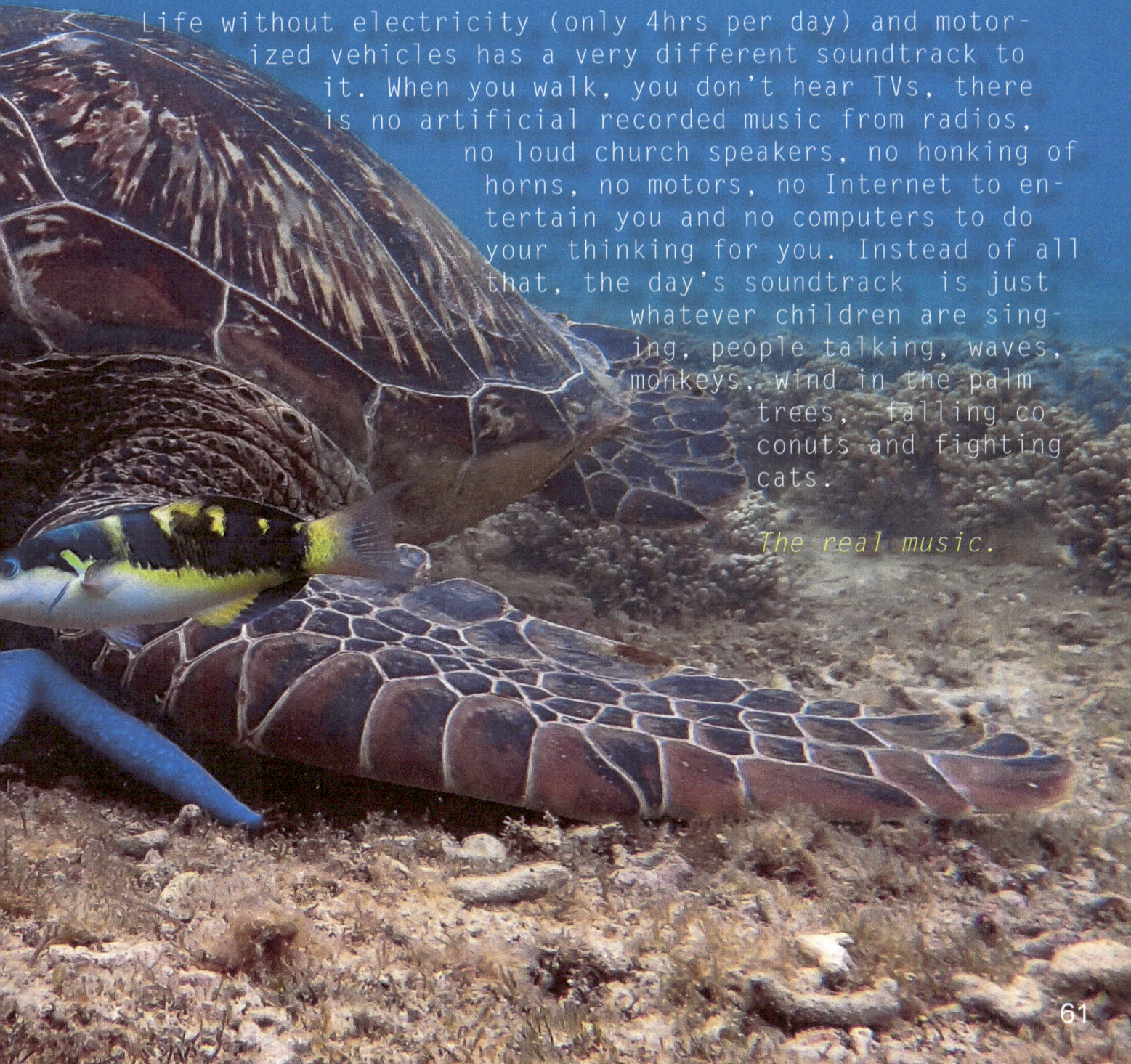

» Apo Island

This one mile-long island is one of the first and best community-organized marine sanctuaries in the world. It sparked the creation of 700+ other marine sanctuaries around the Philippines. On the edge of fishing crisis due to dynamite and cyanide fishing in the 80's, the resident fishermen created a no-take sanctuary zone which served as a nursery to stock the surrounding area. The resulting abundance and diversity of marine animals led to increase in tourism and prompted the Philippine government to create hundreds more sanctuaries.

Life without electricity (only 4hrs per day) and motorized vehicles has a very different soundtrack to it. When you walk, you don't hear TVs, there is no artificial recorded music from radios, no loud church speakers, no honking of horns, no motors, no Internet to entertain you and no computers to do your thinking for you. Instead of all that, the day's soundtrack is just whatever children are singing, people talking, waves, monkeys, wind in the palm trees, falling coconuts and fighting cats.

The real music.

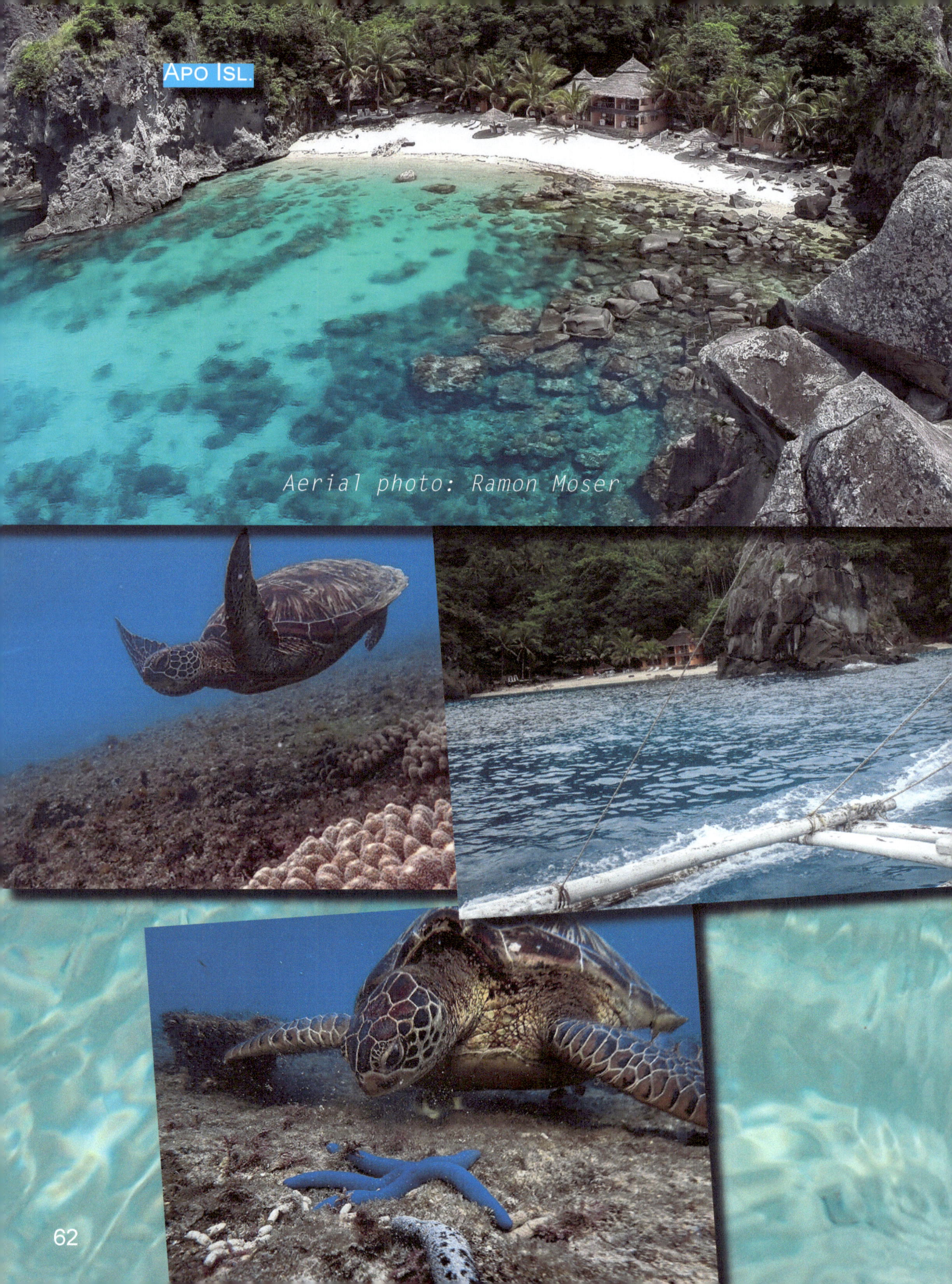

Aerial photo: Ramon Moser

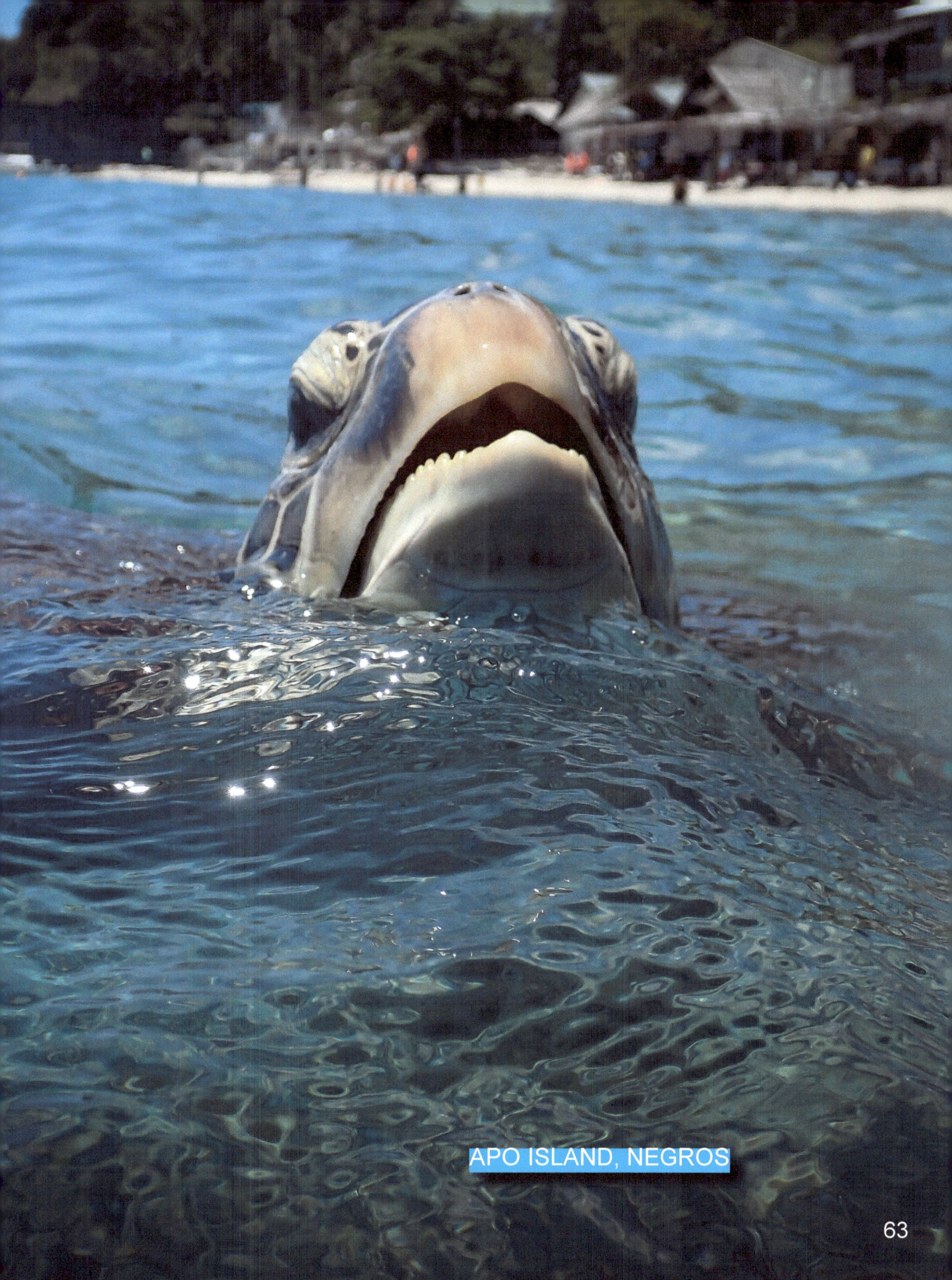

APO ISLAND, NEGROS

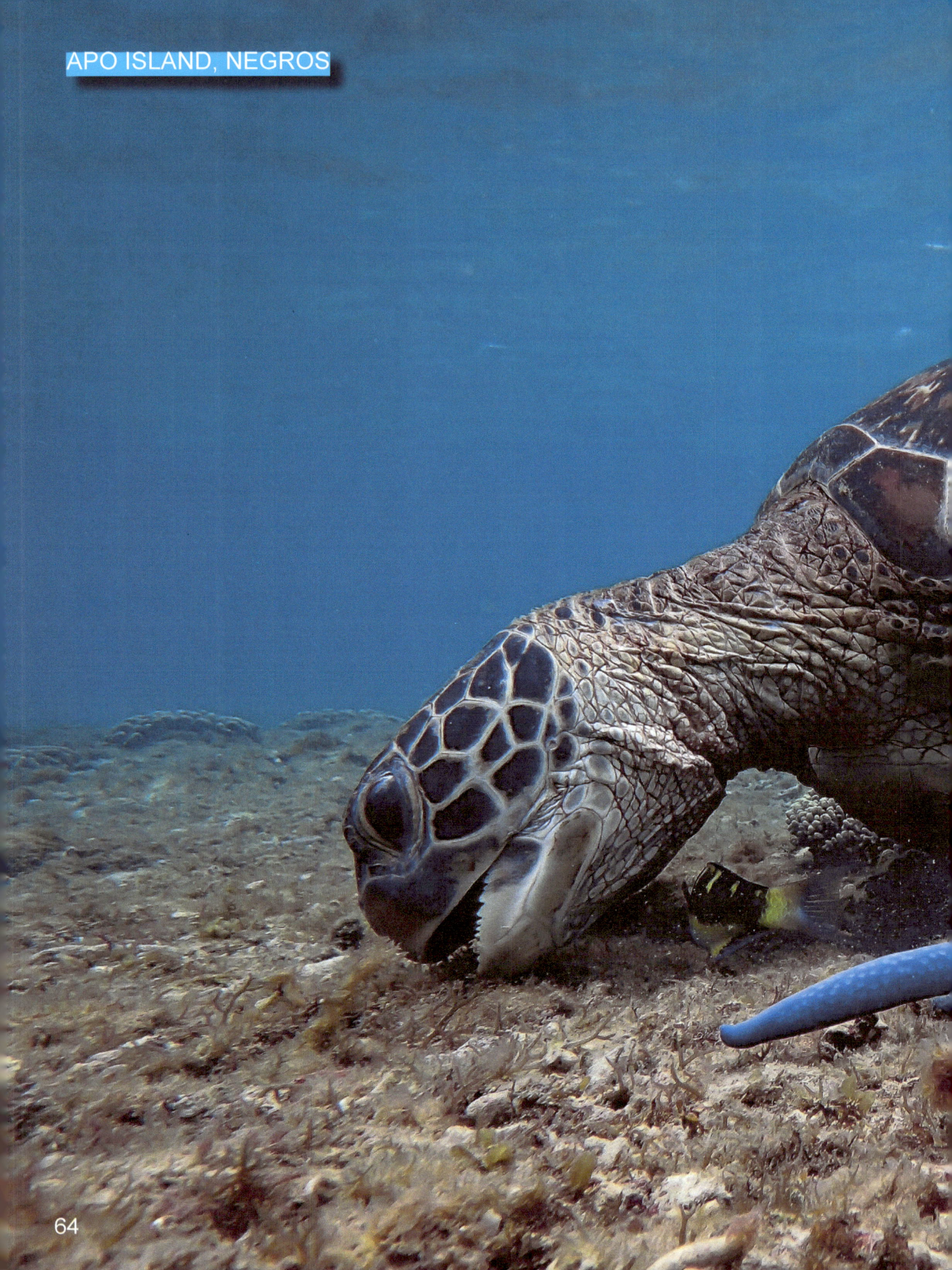

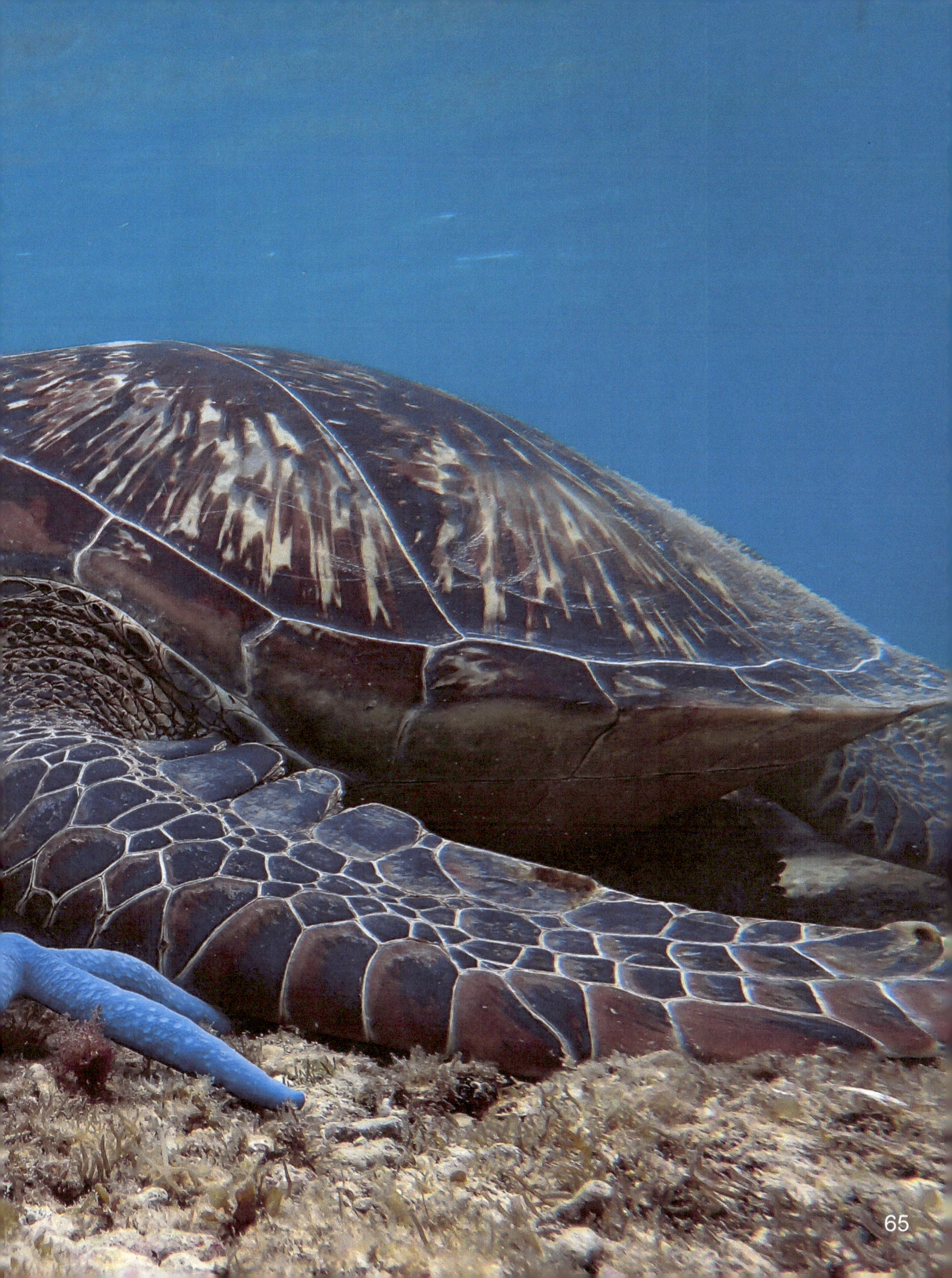

This chapter contains examples of what you can expect to see snorkeling in Moalboal, Cebu. Both beaches of Moalboal (Panagsama and White Beach) are great for snorkeling. It's a wall dive. On a low tide, you can go chest deep and the wall drops off almost vertically into the depths. It's like this all over Moalboal. But you don't have to go into the great depths to see the corals and the fish in the photos. The vast majority of those photos were taken around 10' deep and you don't even have to know how to swim in order to see that stuff.

» *Sardine Run*

There are huge clouds of sardines 24/7 in Panagsama Beach, Moalboal. Ask anybody who lives there to show you the exact spot. These sardines are only 10' deep, so you don't have to be a strong swimmer to see them.

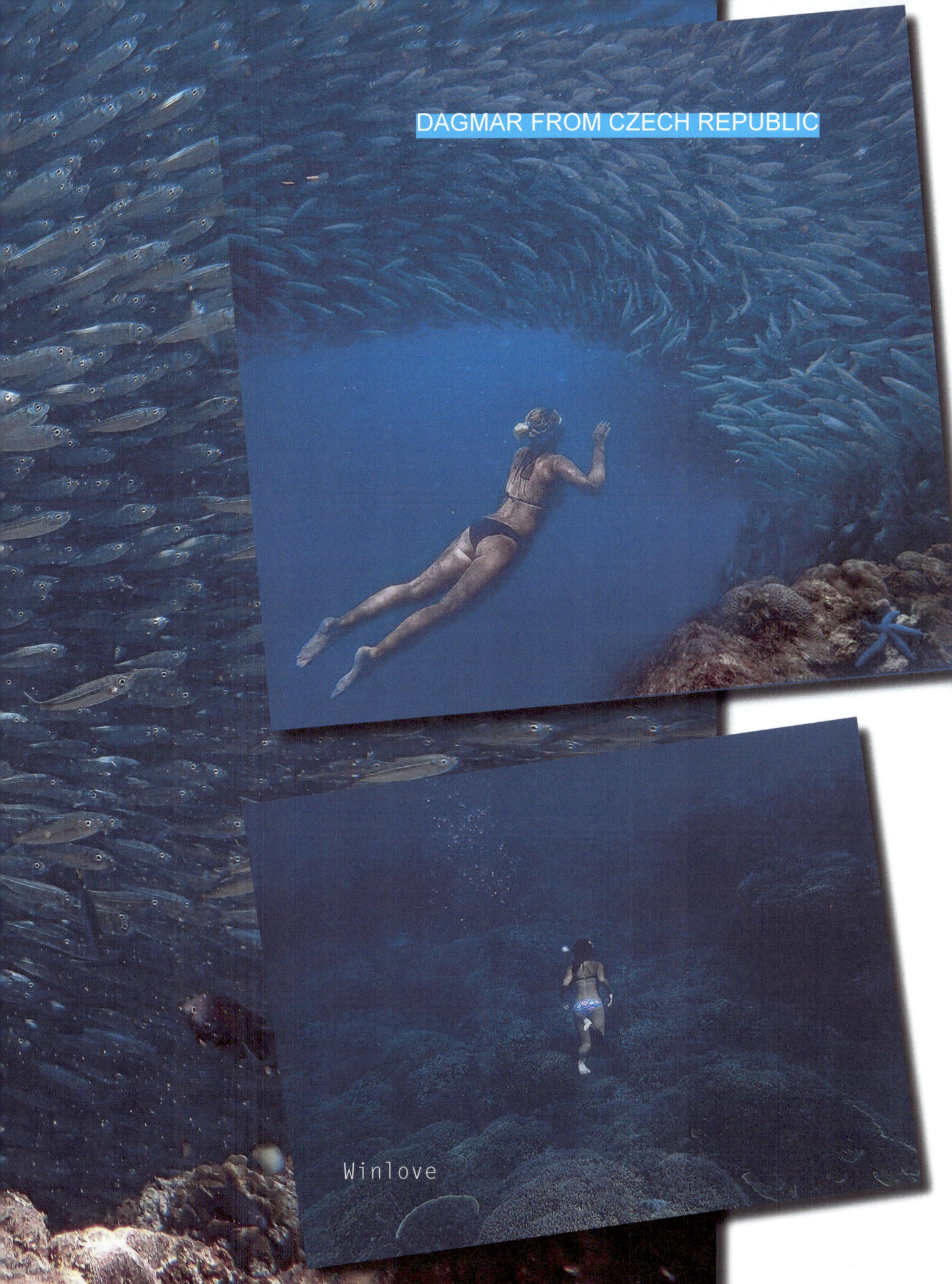

Winlove

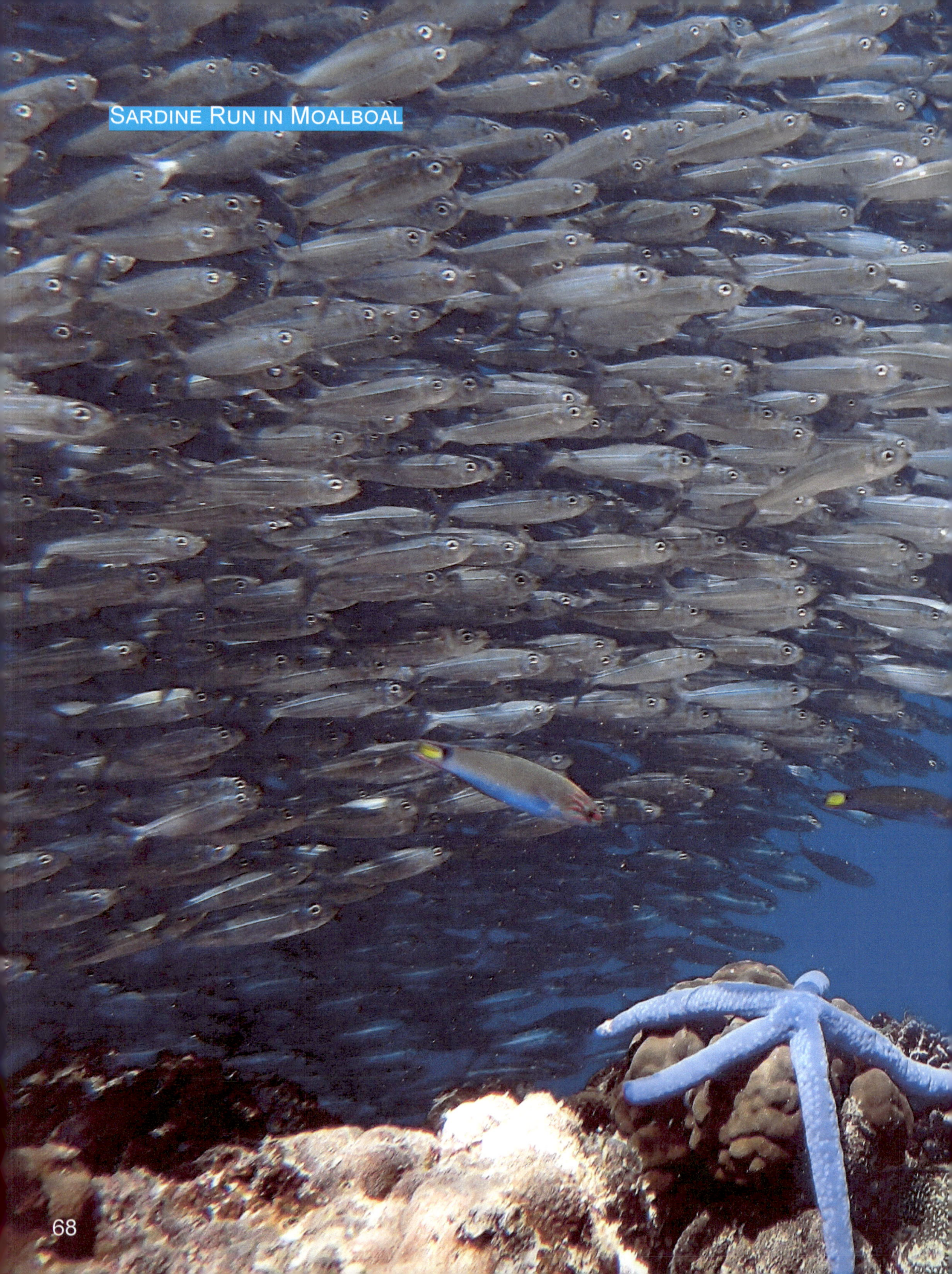

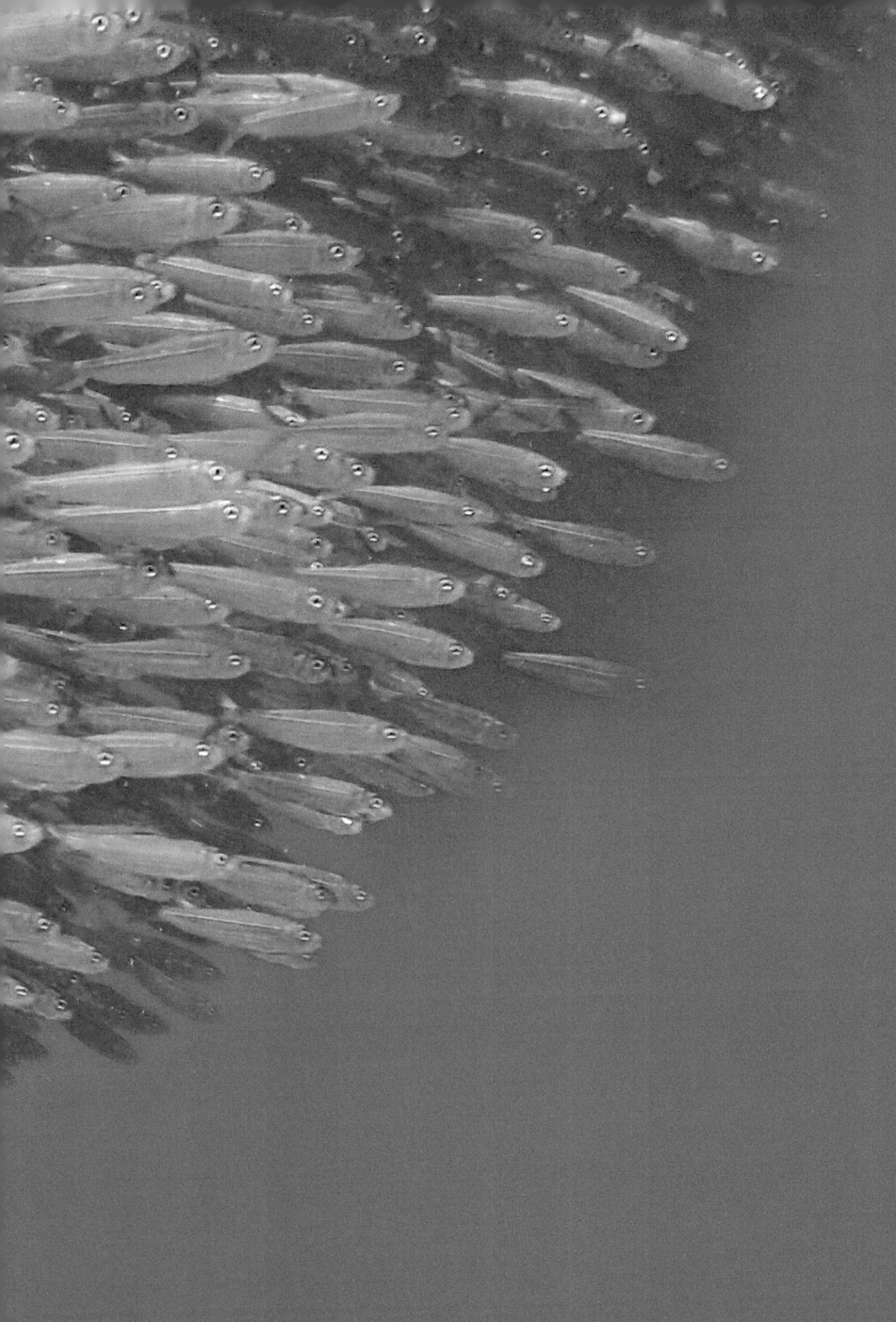

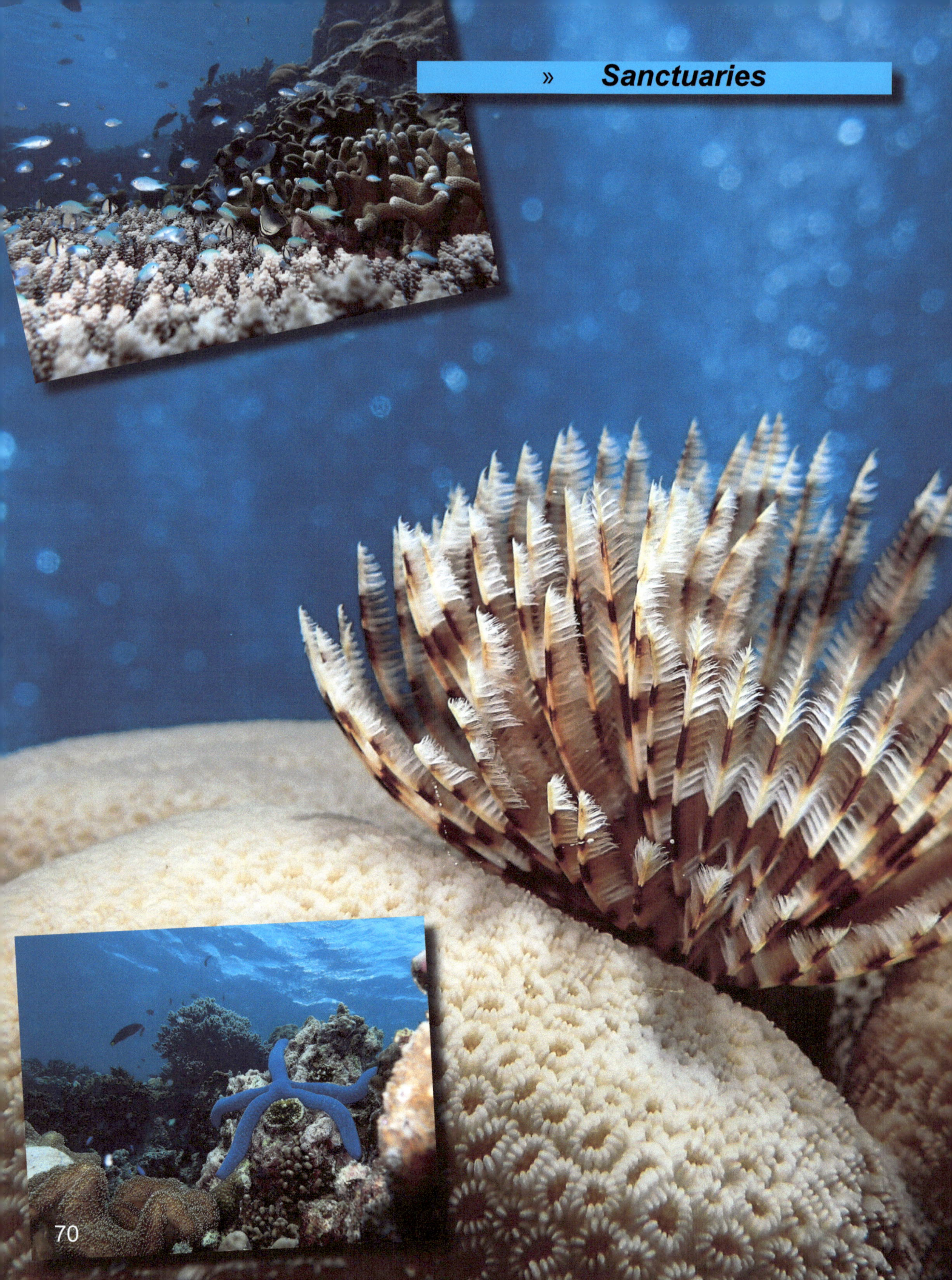

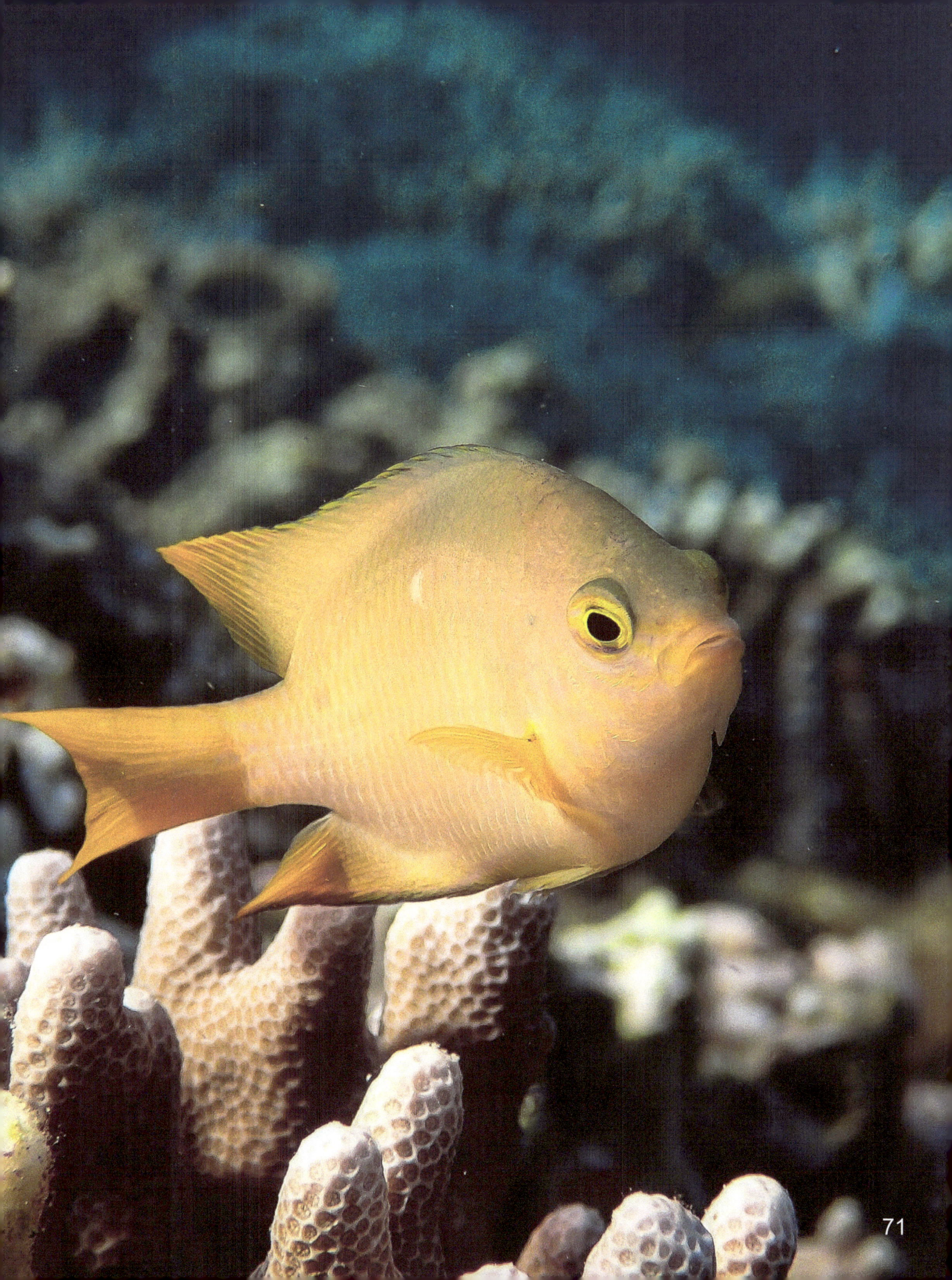

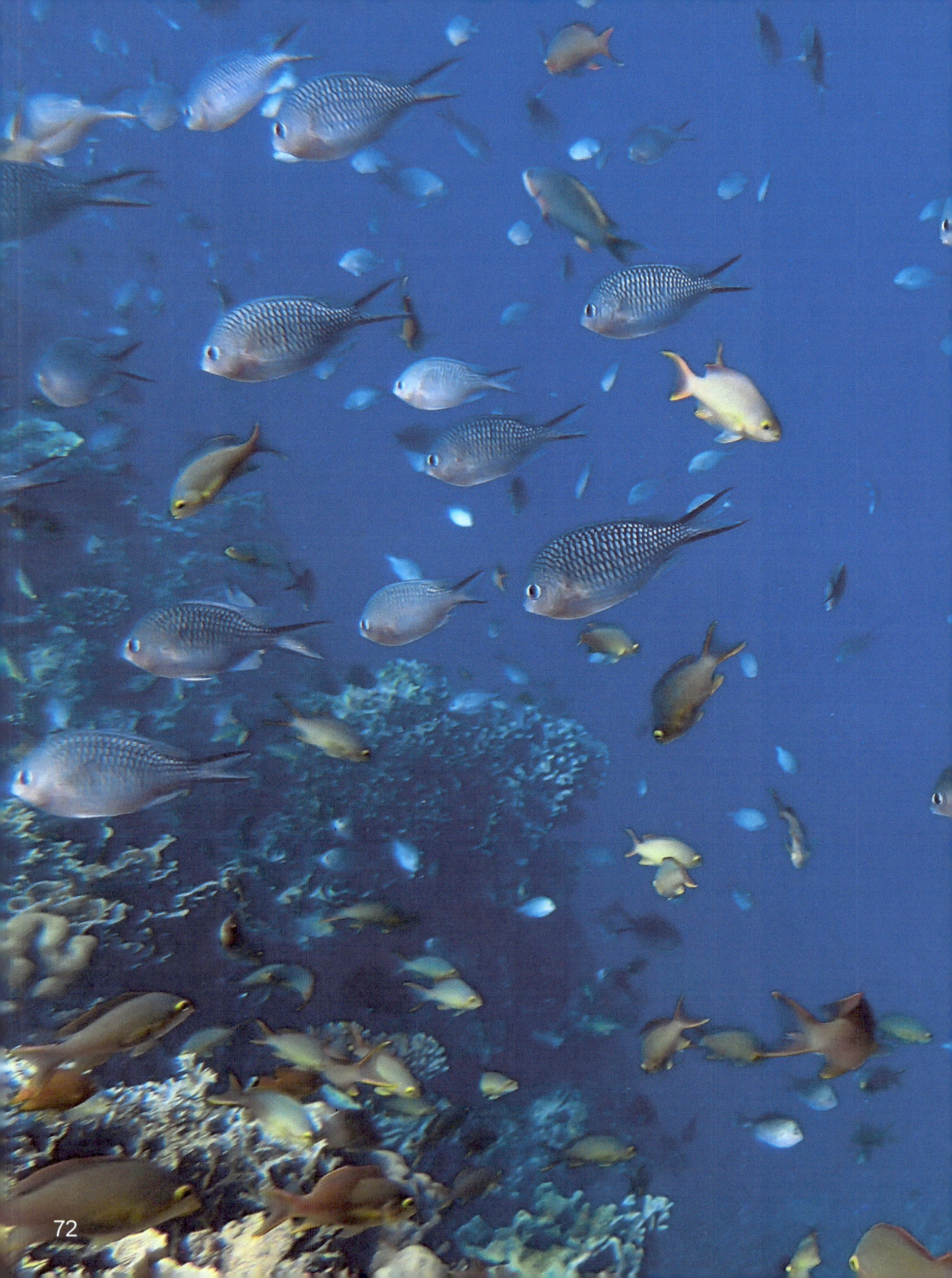

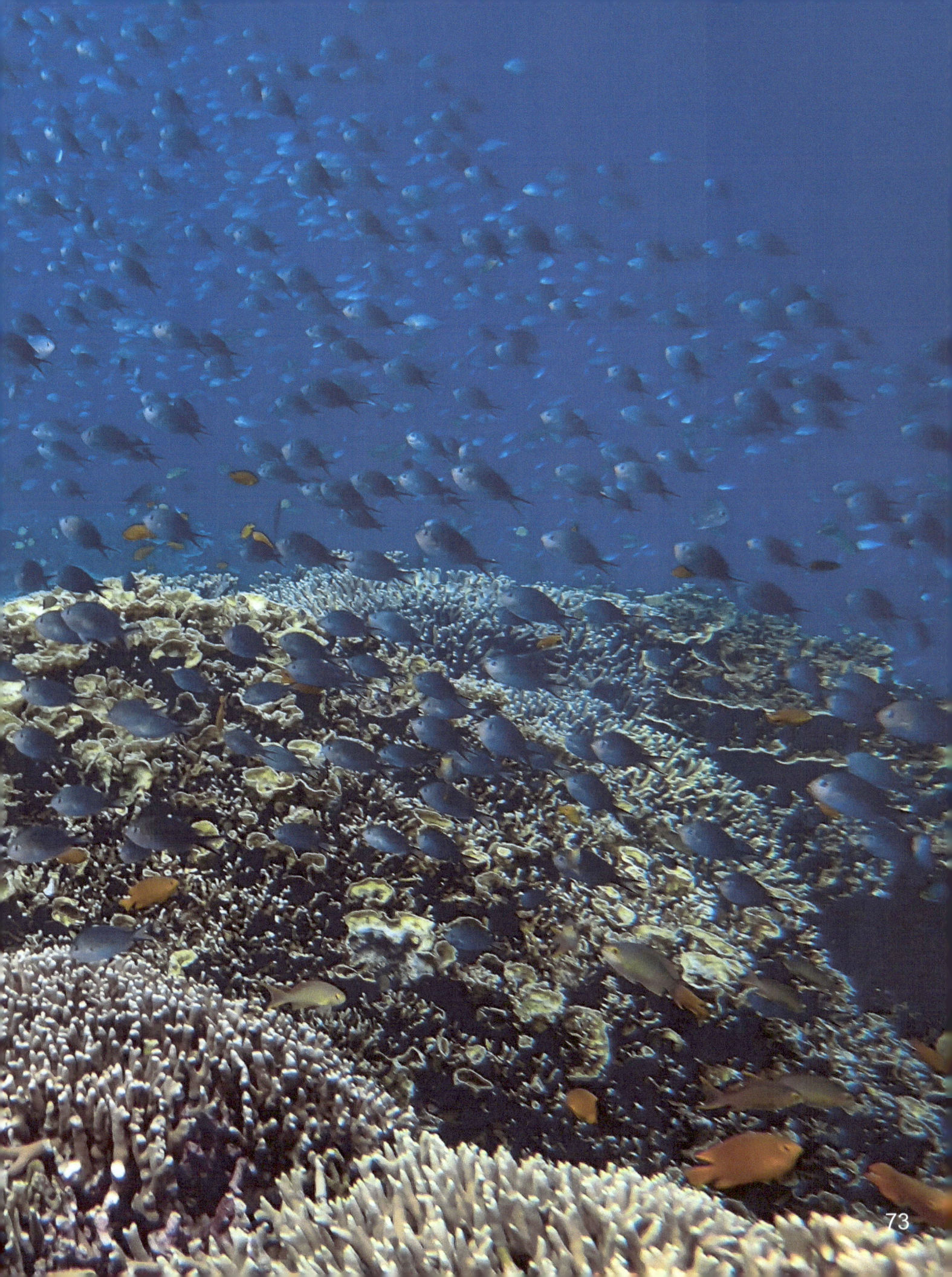

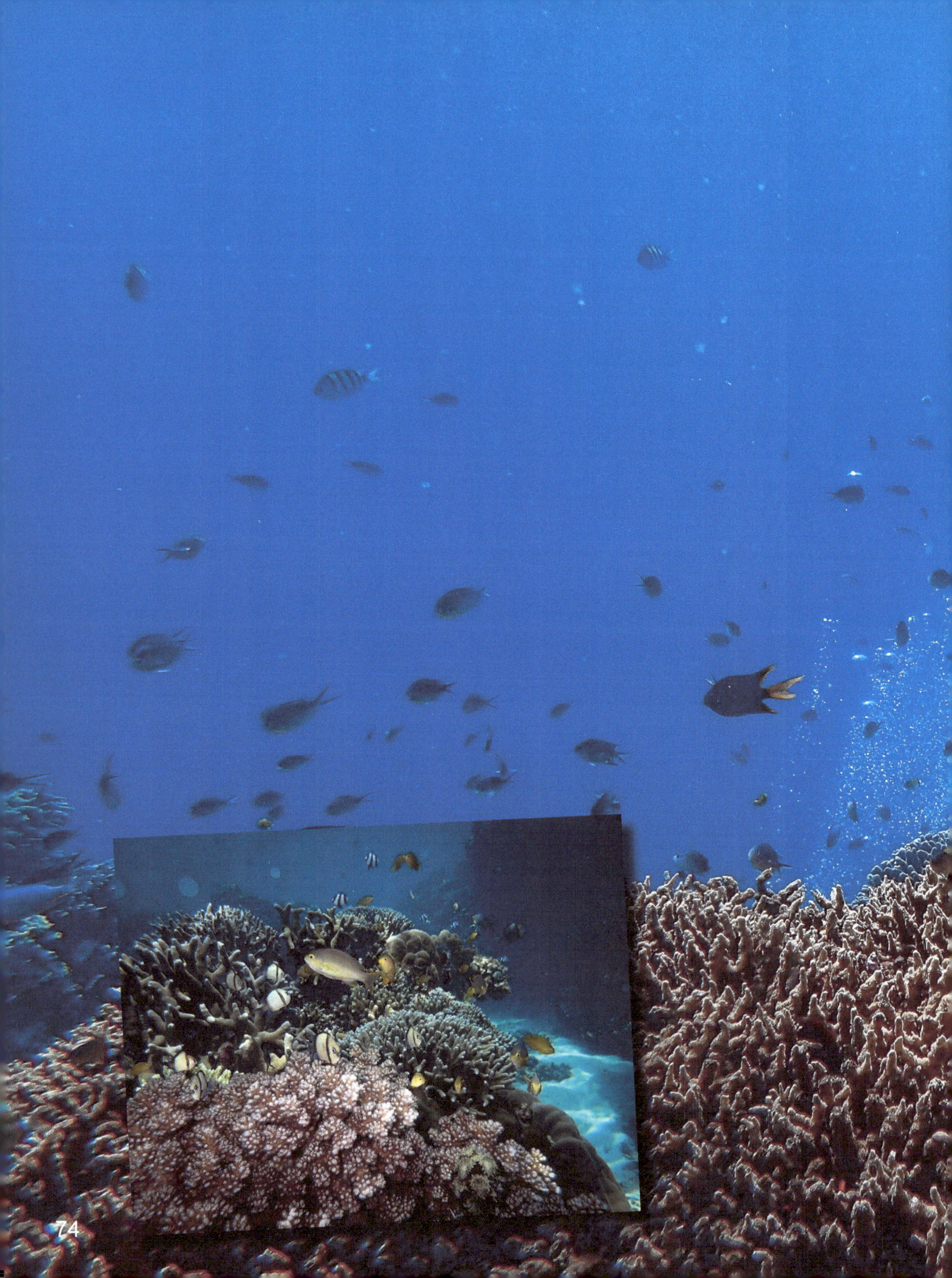

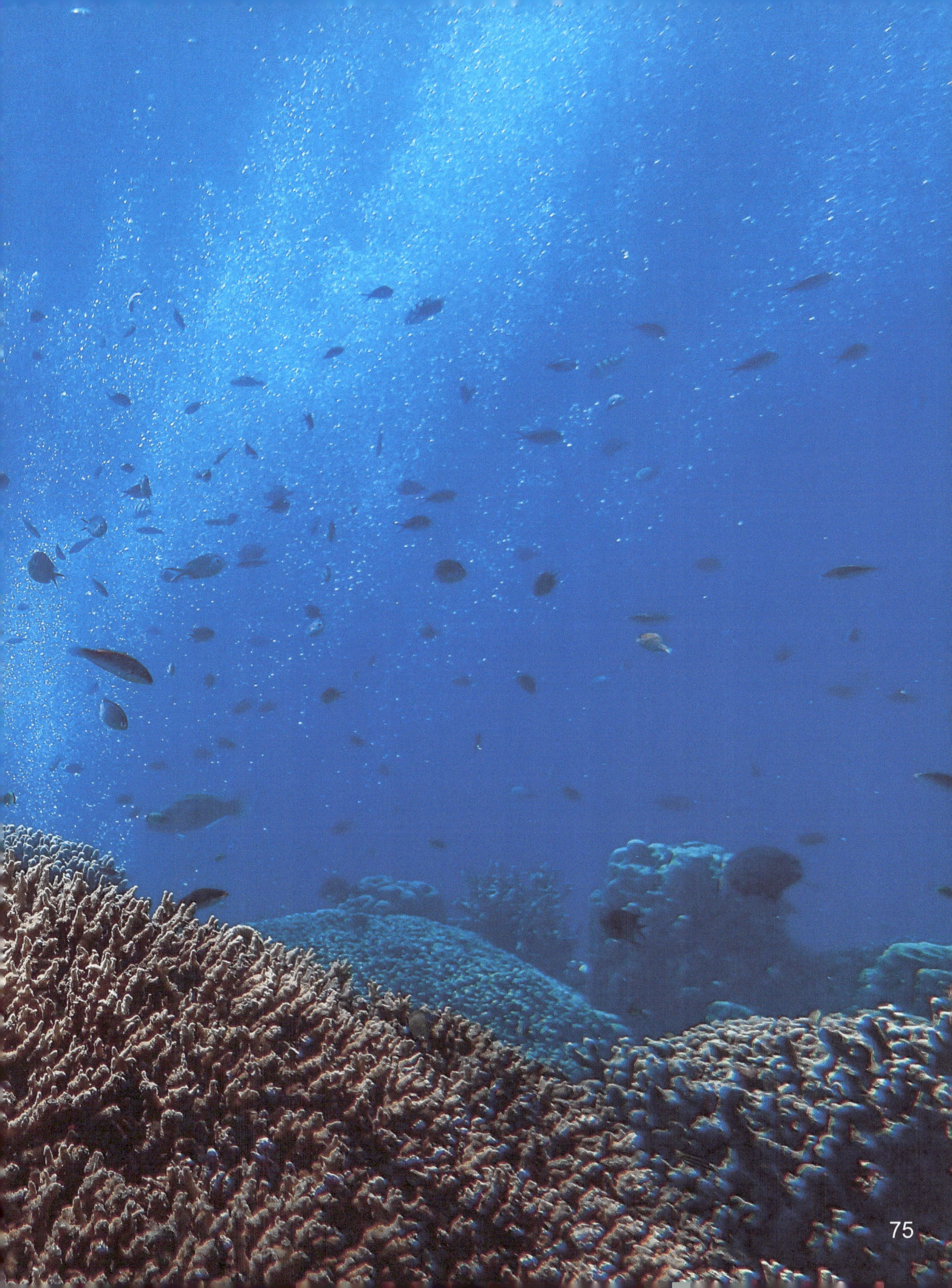

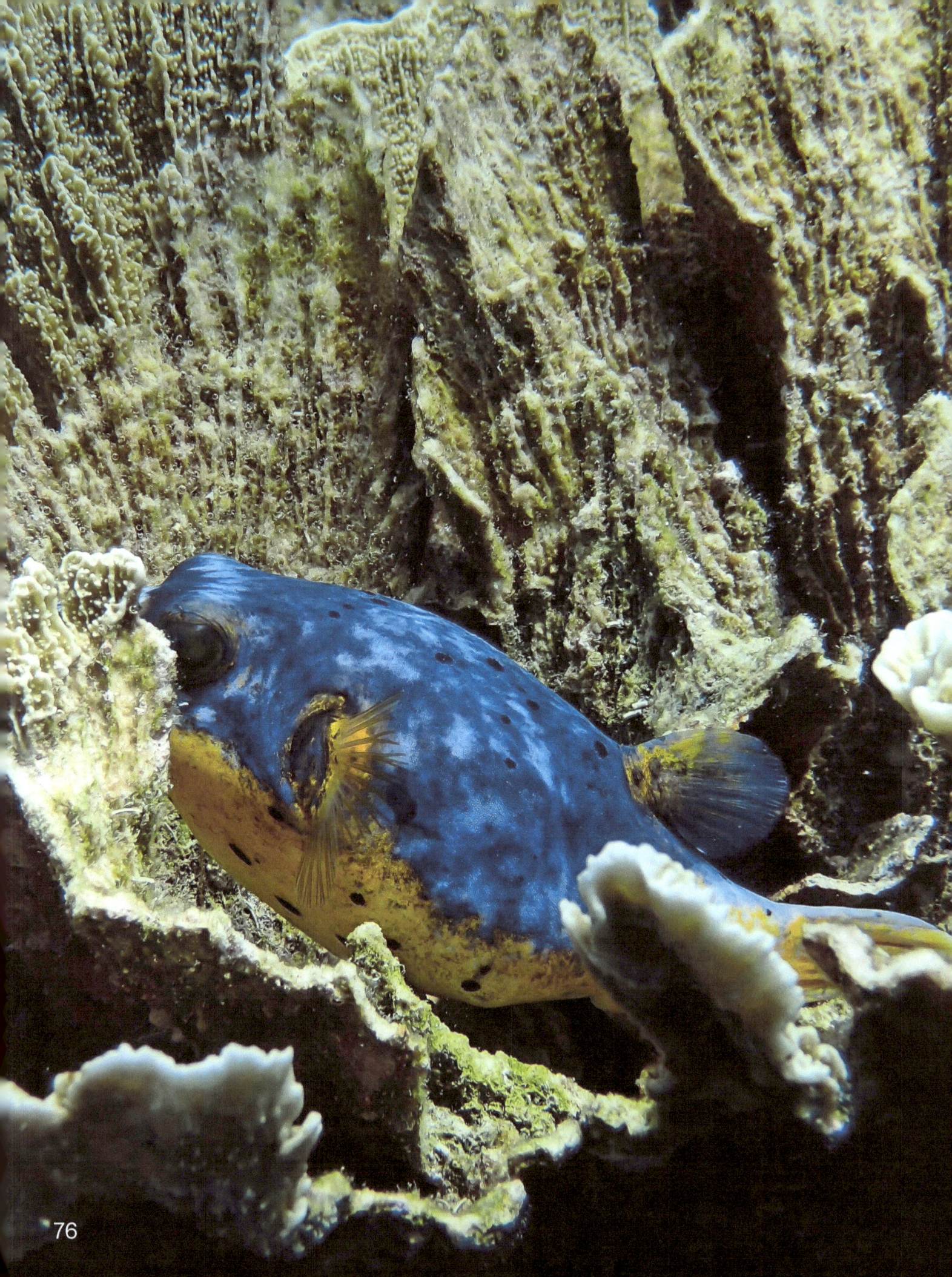

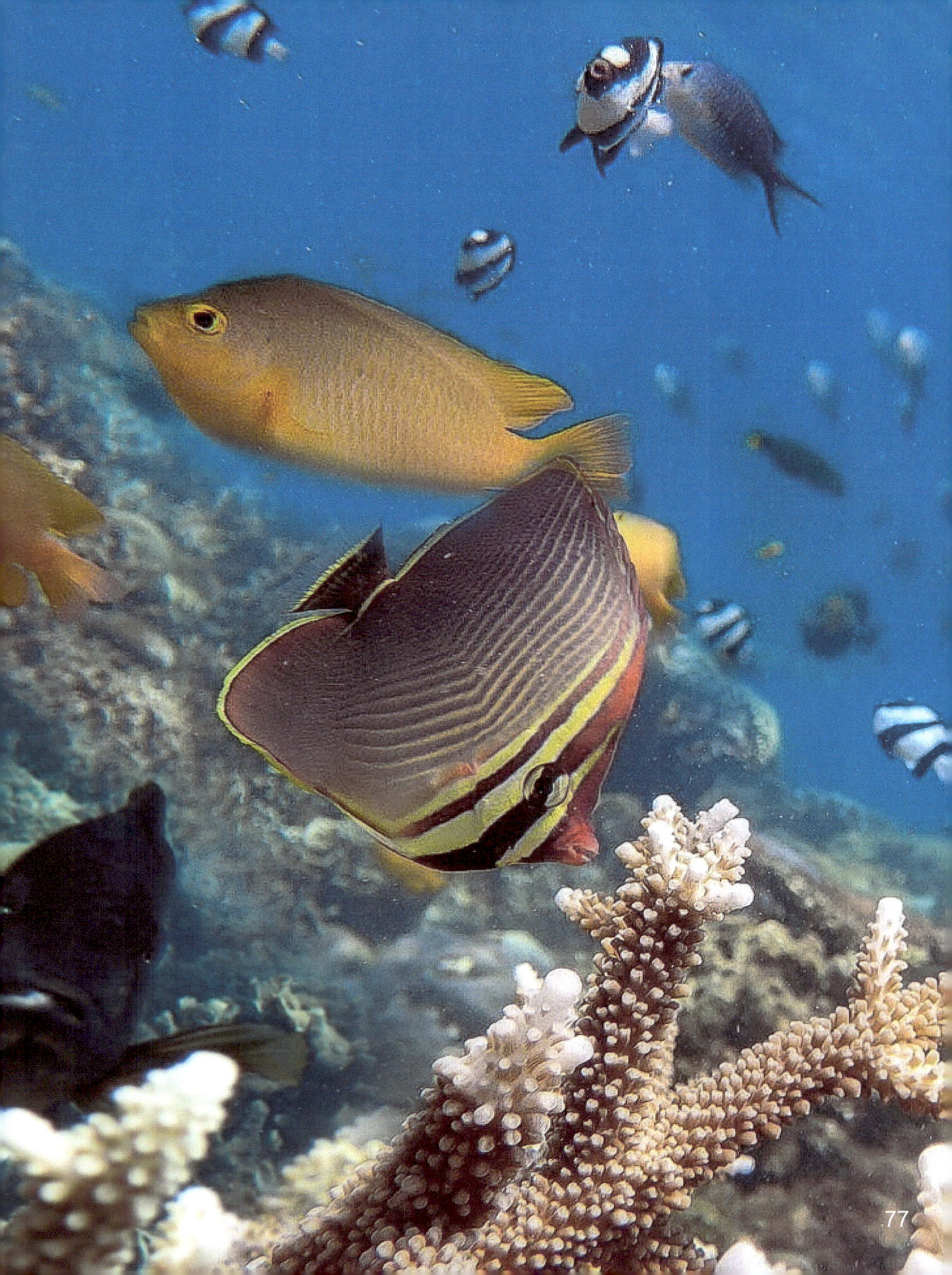

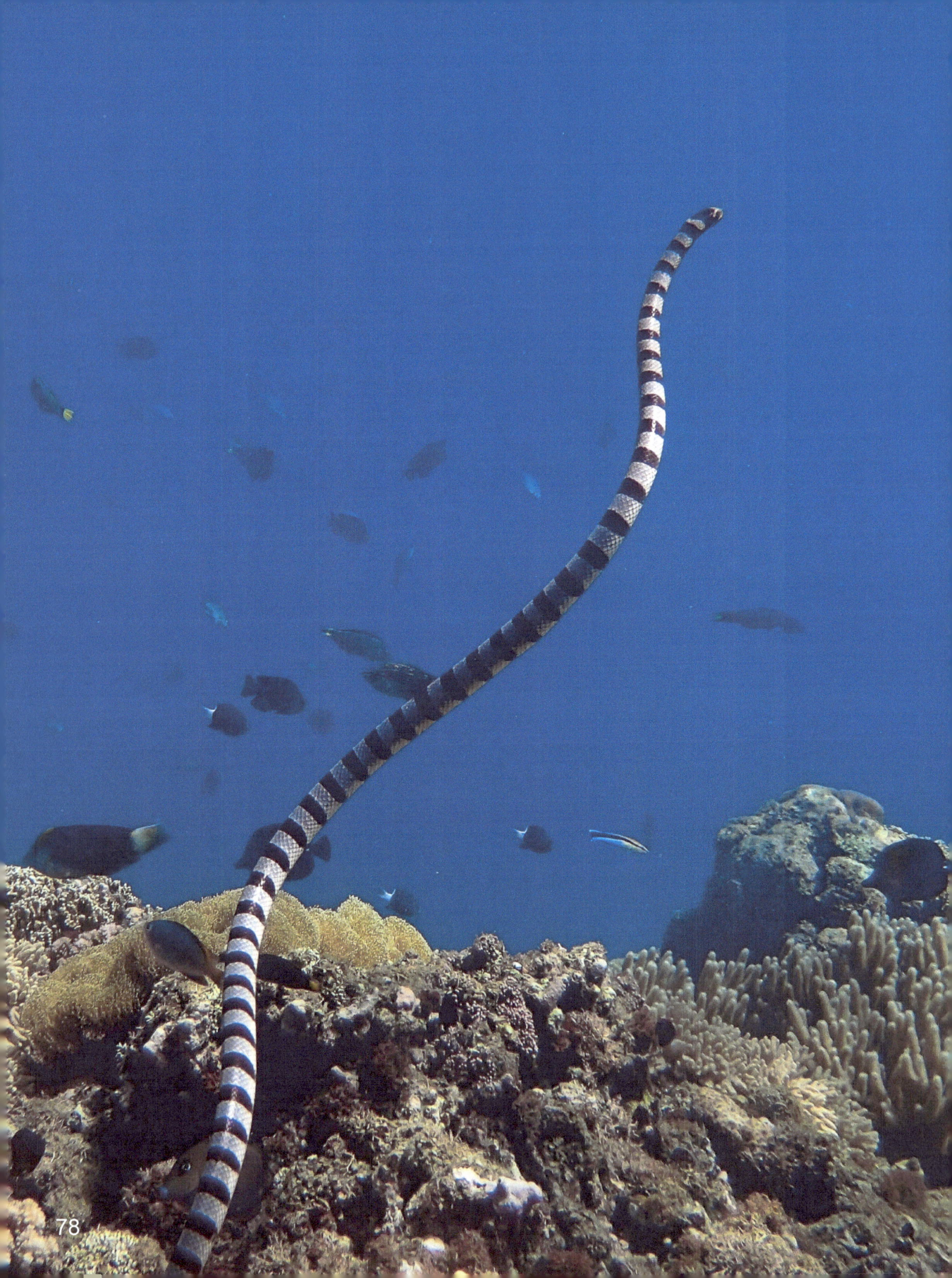

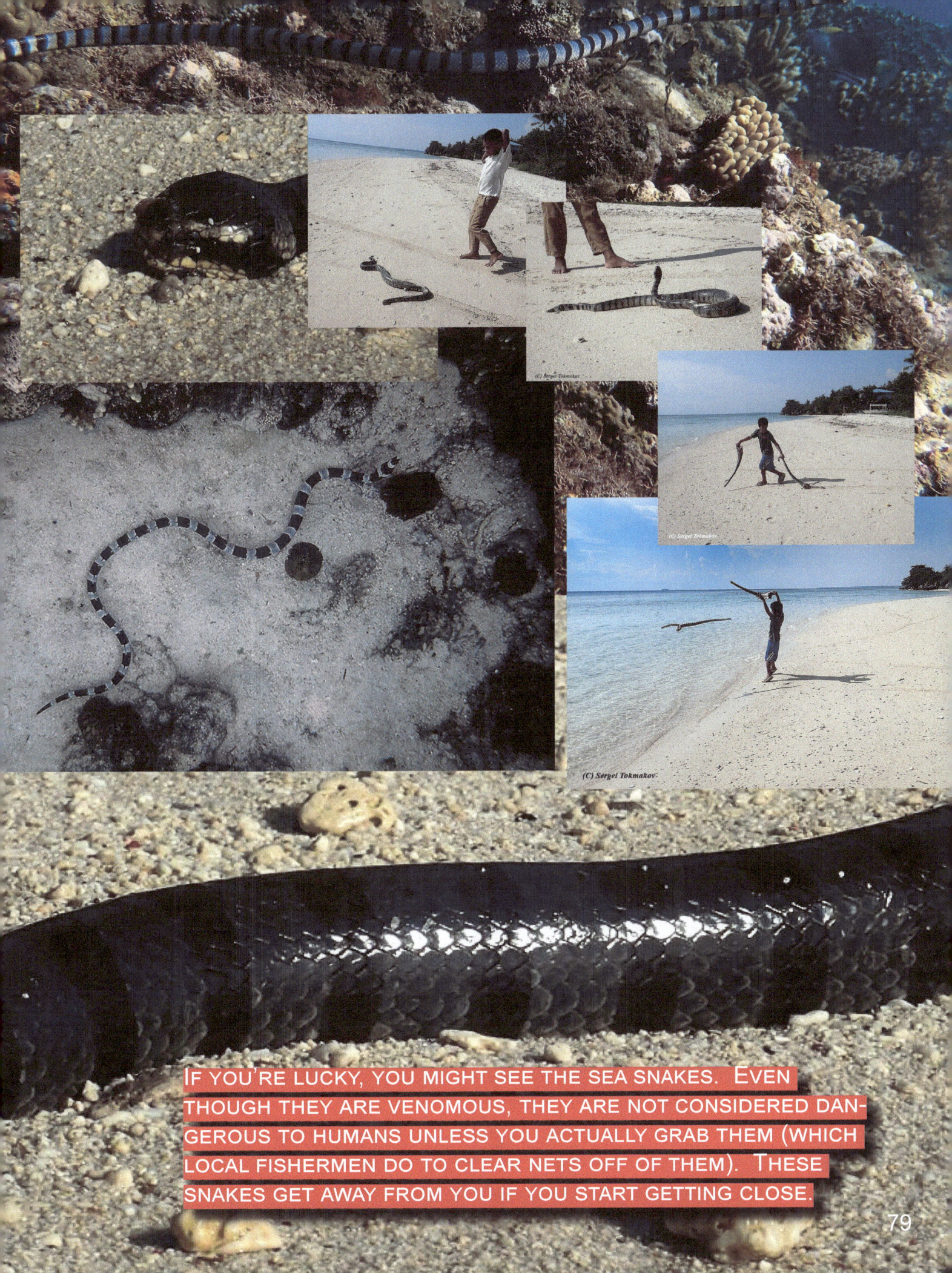

(C) Sergei Tokmakov

IF YOU'RE LUCKY, YOU MIGHT SEE THE SEA SNAKES. EVEN THOUGH THEY ARE VENOMOUS, THEY ARE NOT CONSIDERED DANGEROUS TO HUMANS UNLESS YOU ACTUALLY GRAB THEM (WHICH LOCAL FISHERMEN DO TO CLEAR NETS OFF OF THEM). THESE SNAKES GET AWAY FROM YOU IF YOU START GETTING CLOSE.

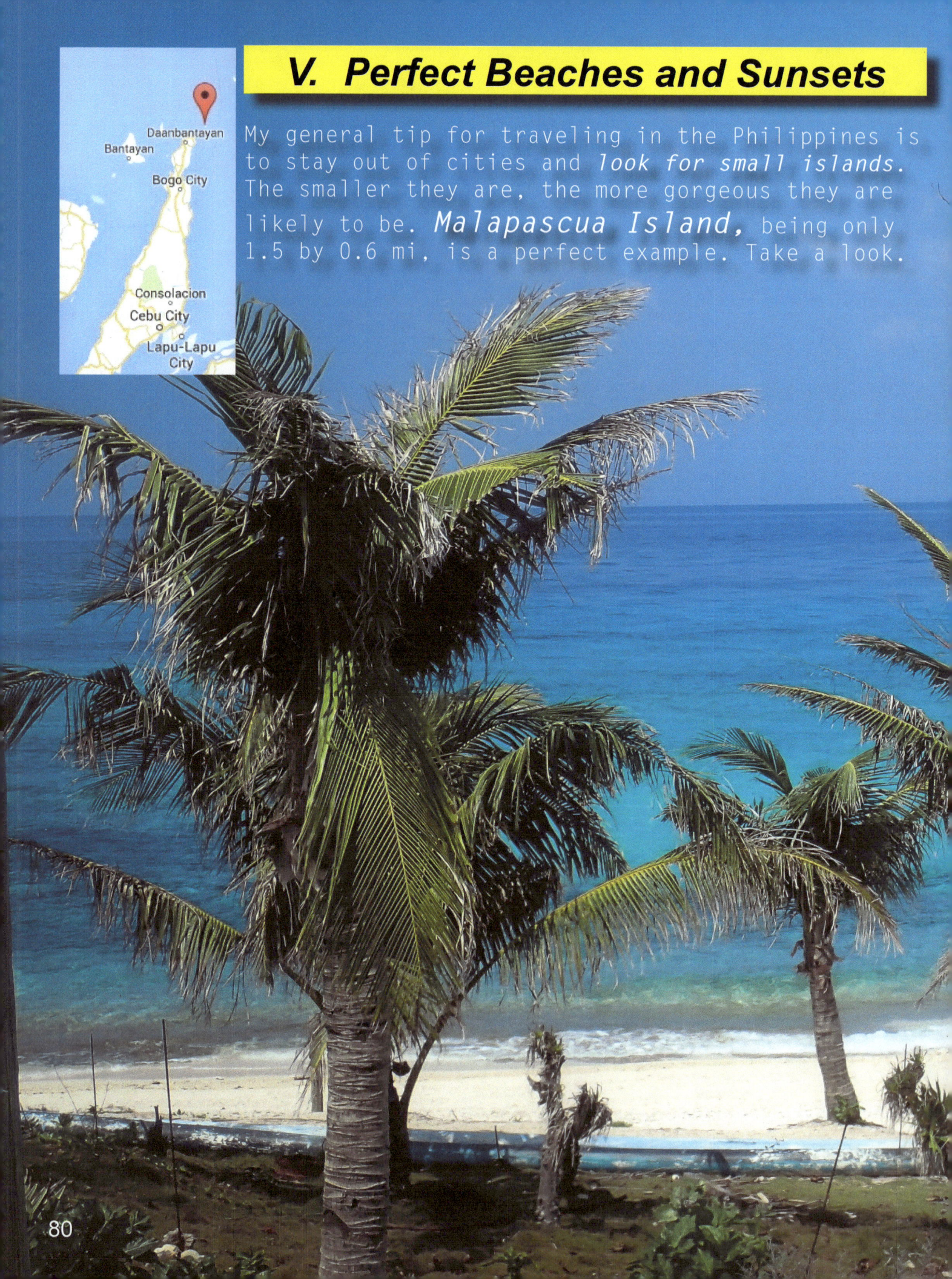

V. Perfect Beaches and Sunsets

My general tip for traveling in the Philippines is to stay out of cities and *look for small islands*. The smaller they are, the more gorgeous they are likely to be. *Malapascua Island,* being only 1.5 by 0.6 mi, is a perfect example. Take a look.

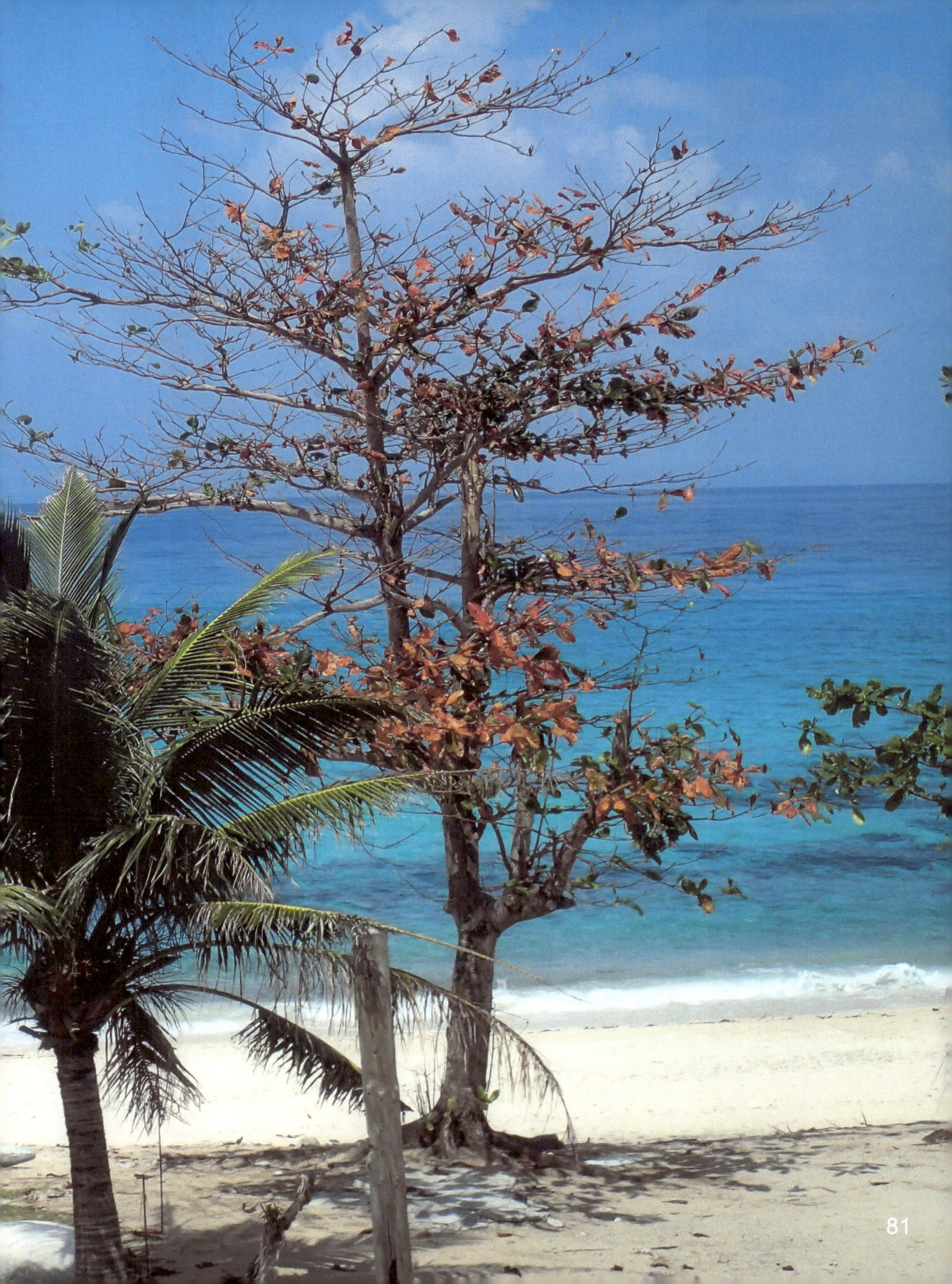

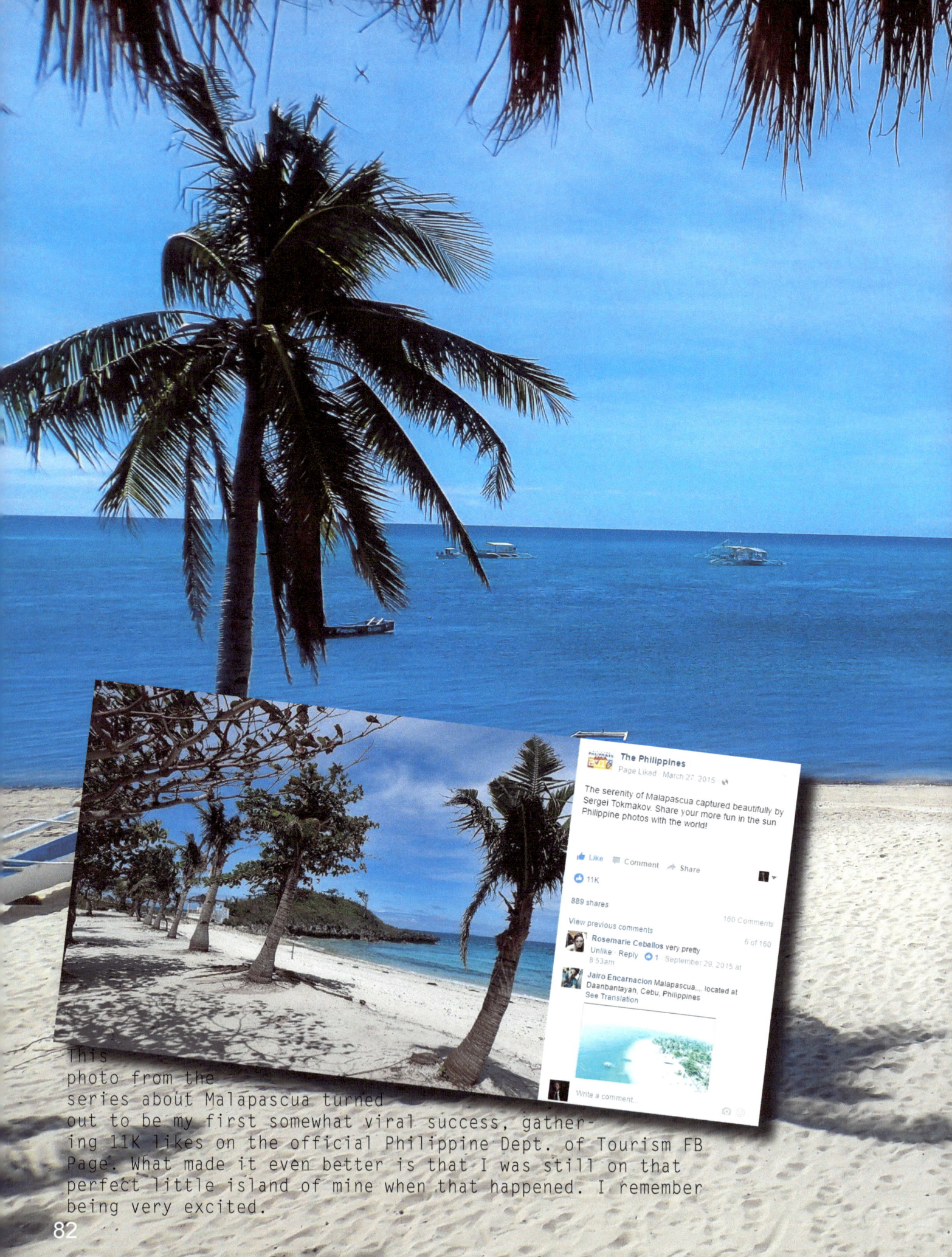

This photo from the series about Malapascua turned out to be my first somewhat viral success, gathering 11K likes on the official Philippine Dept. of Tourism FB Page. What made it even better is that I was still on that perfect little island of mine when that happened. I remember being very excited.

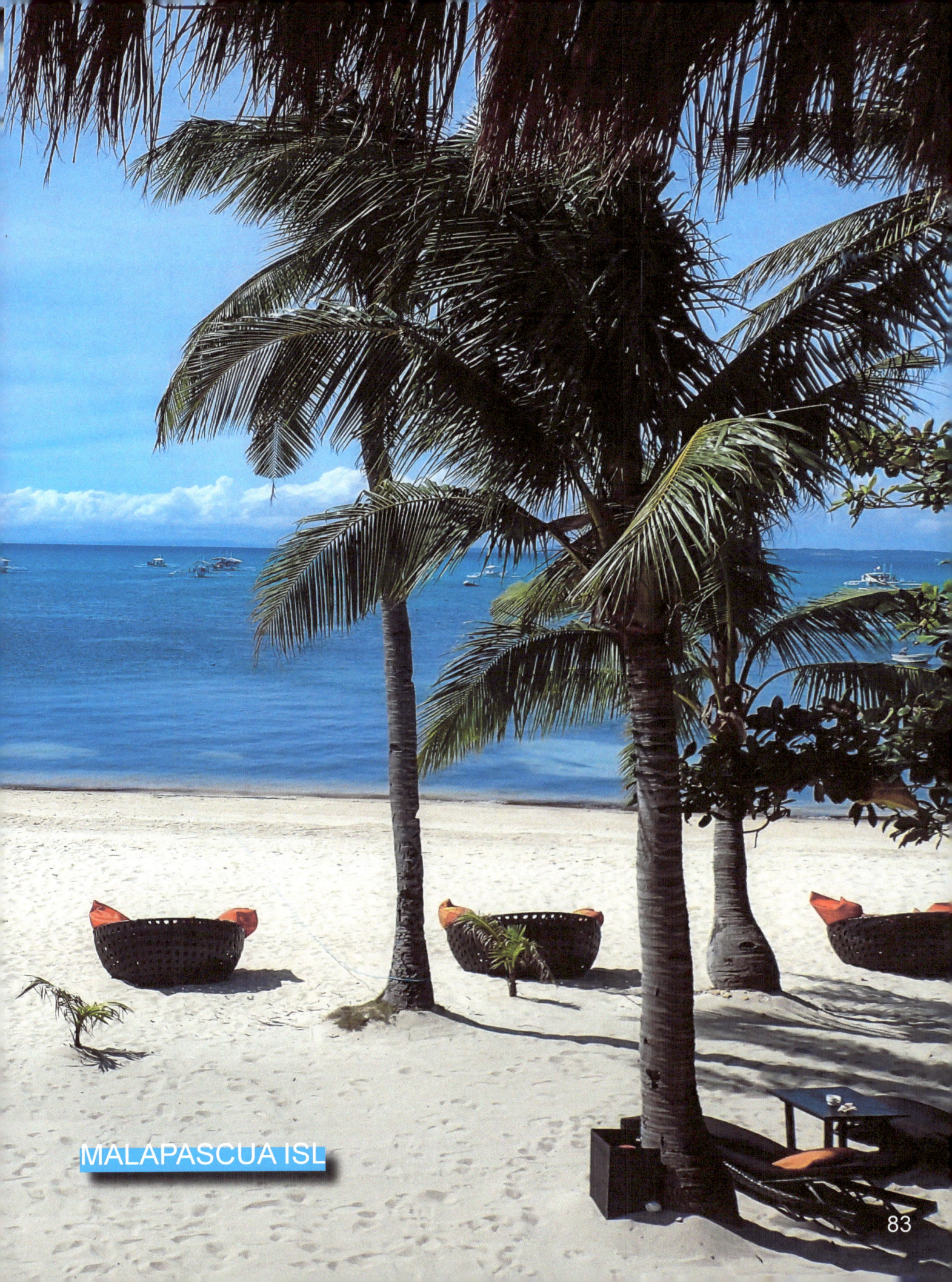

MALAPASCUA ISL

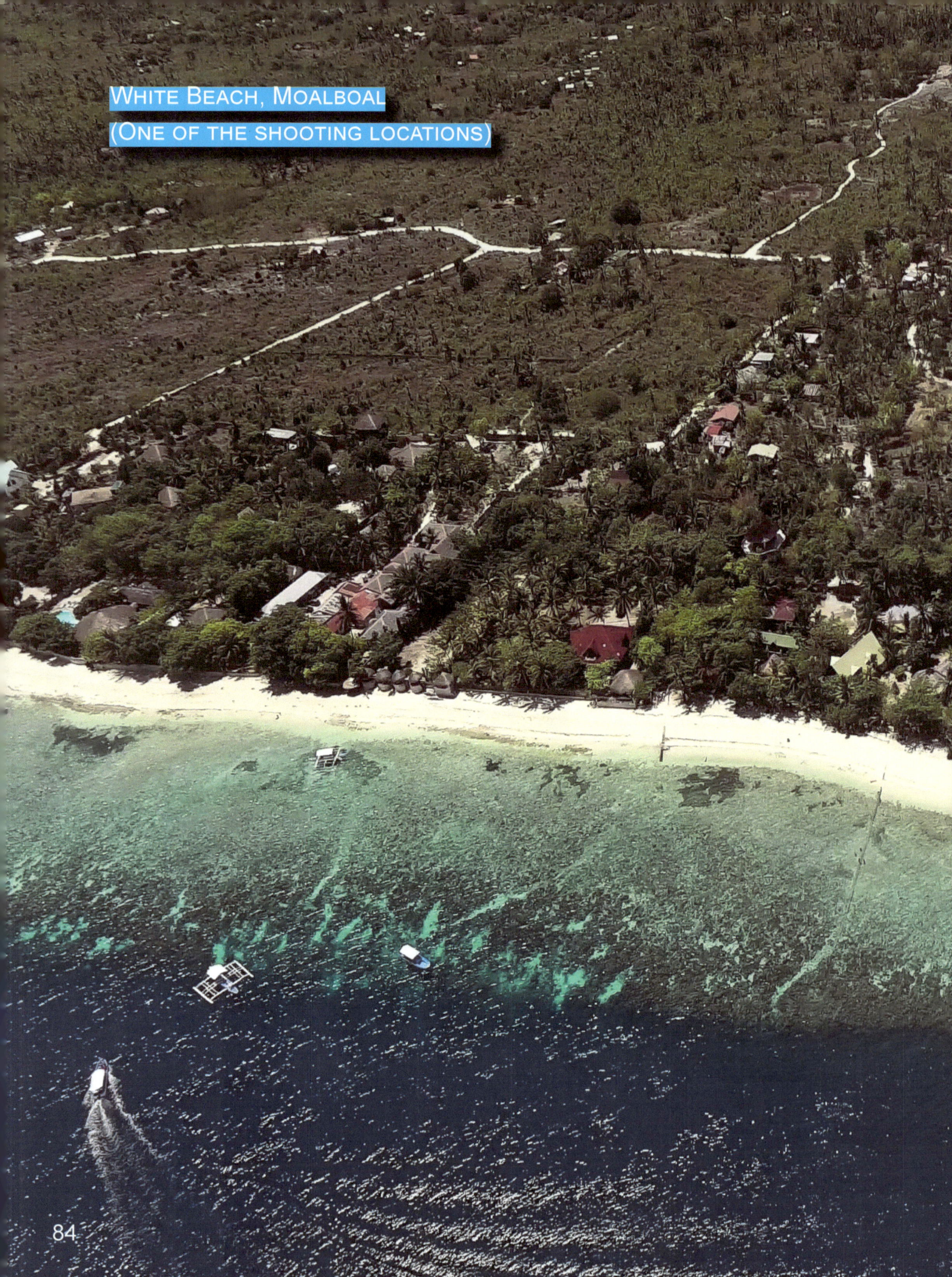

WHITE BEACH, MOALBOAL
(ONE OF THE SHOOTING LOCATIONS)

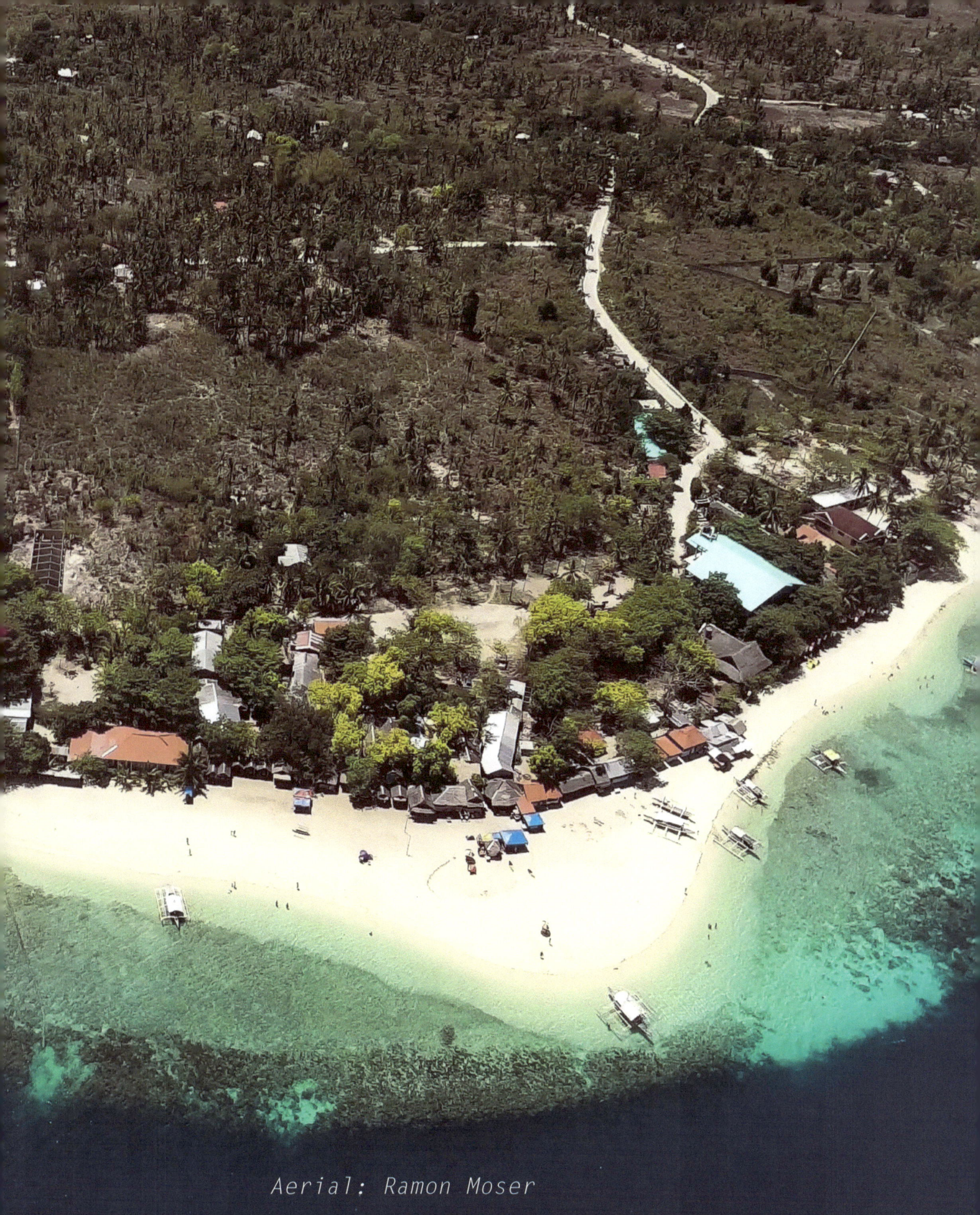

Aerial: Ramon Moser

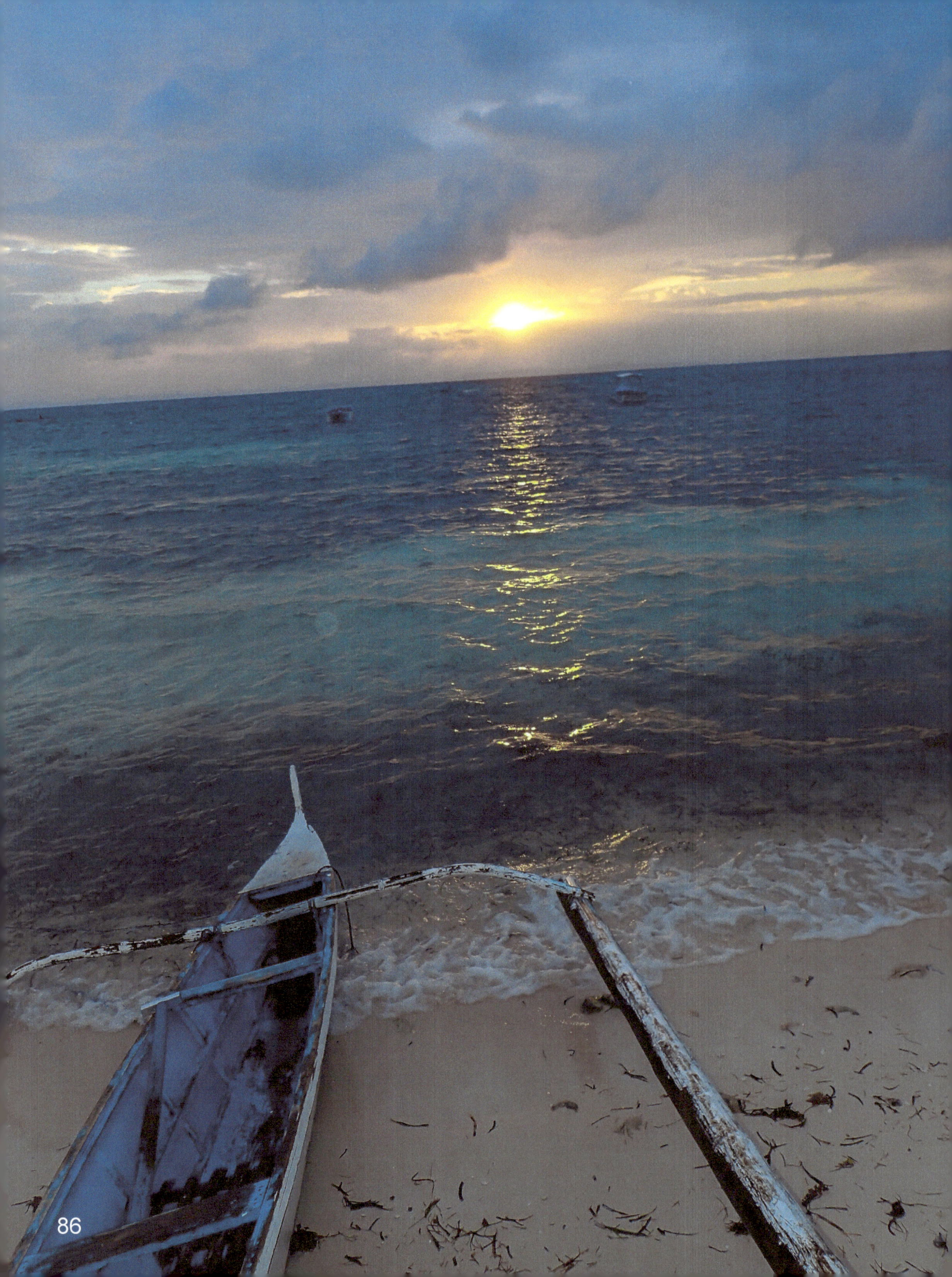

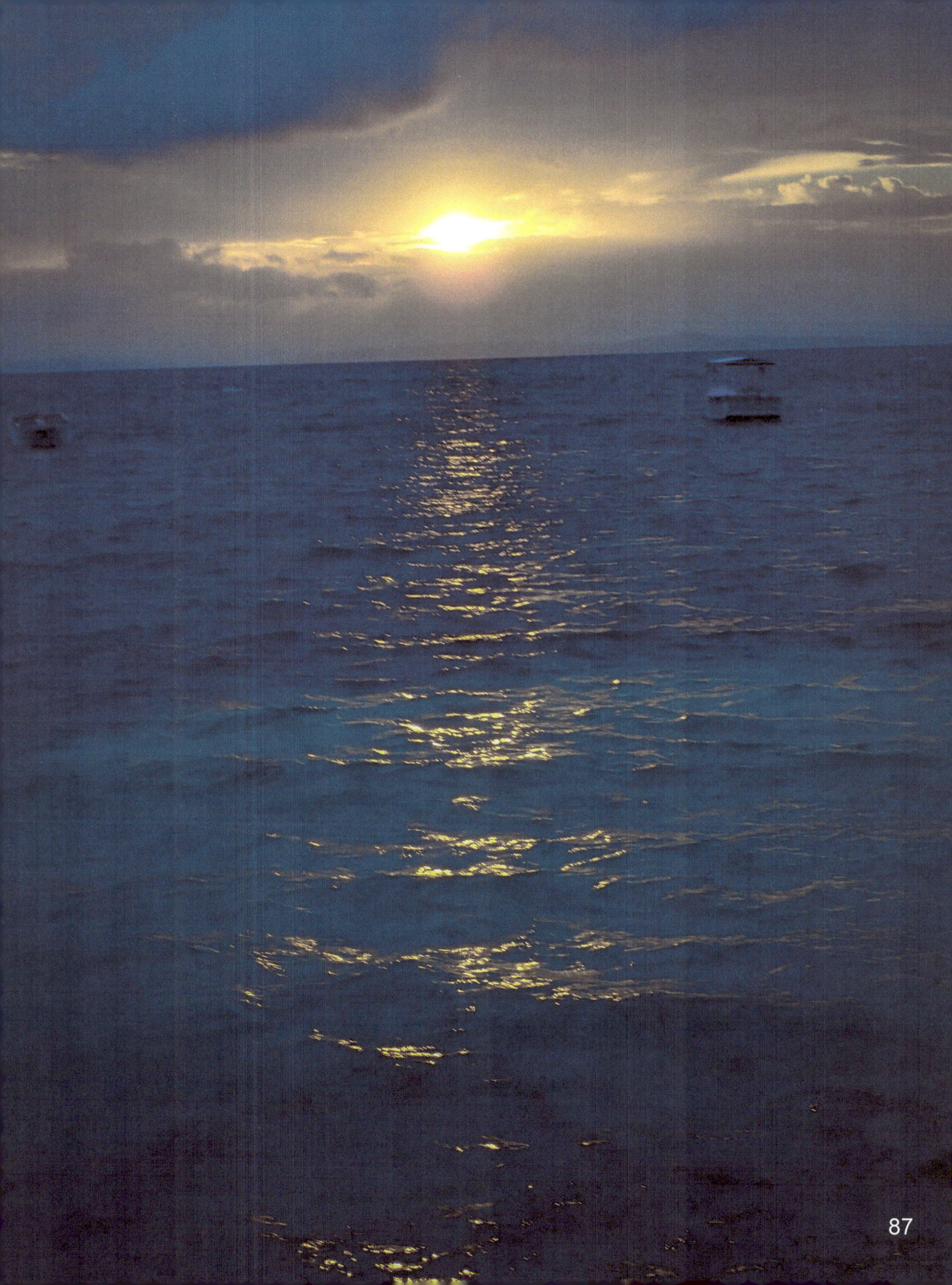

I love waking up and going to sleep looking at this boat from my window in Moalboal.

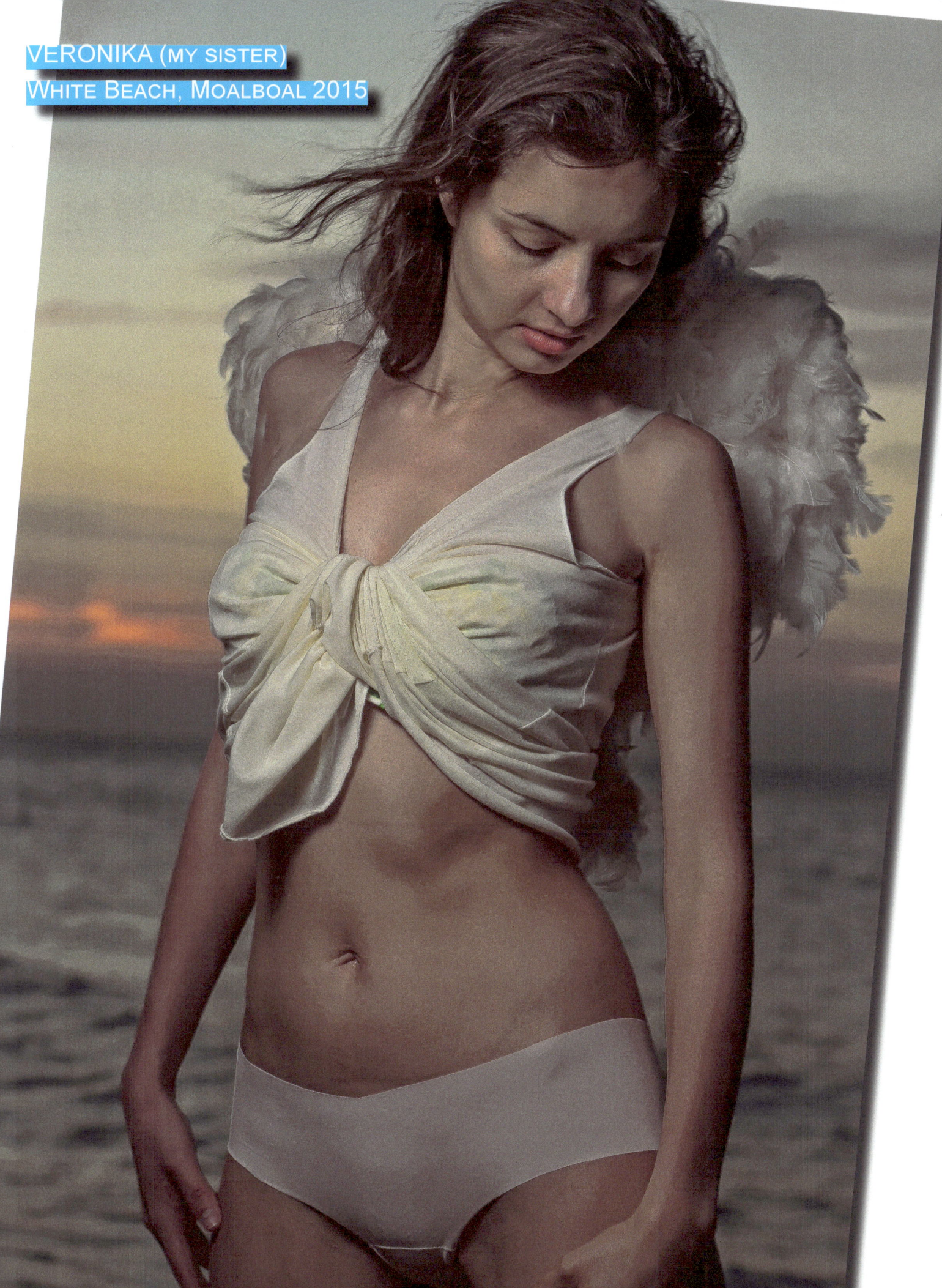

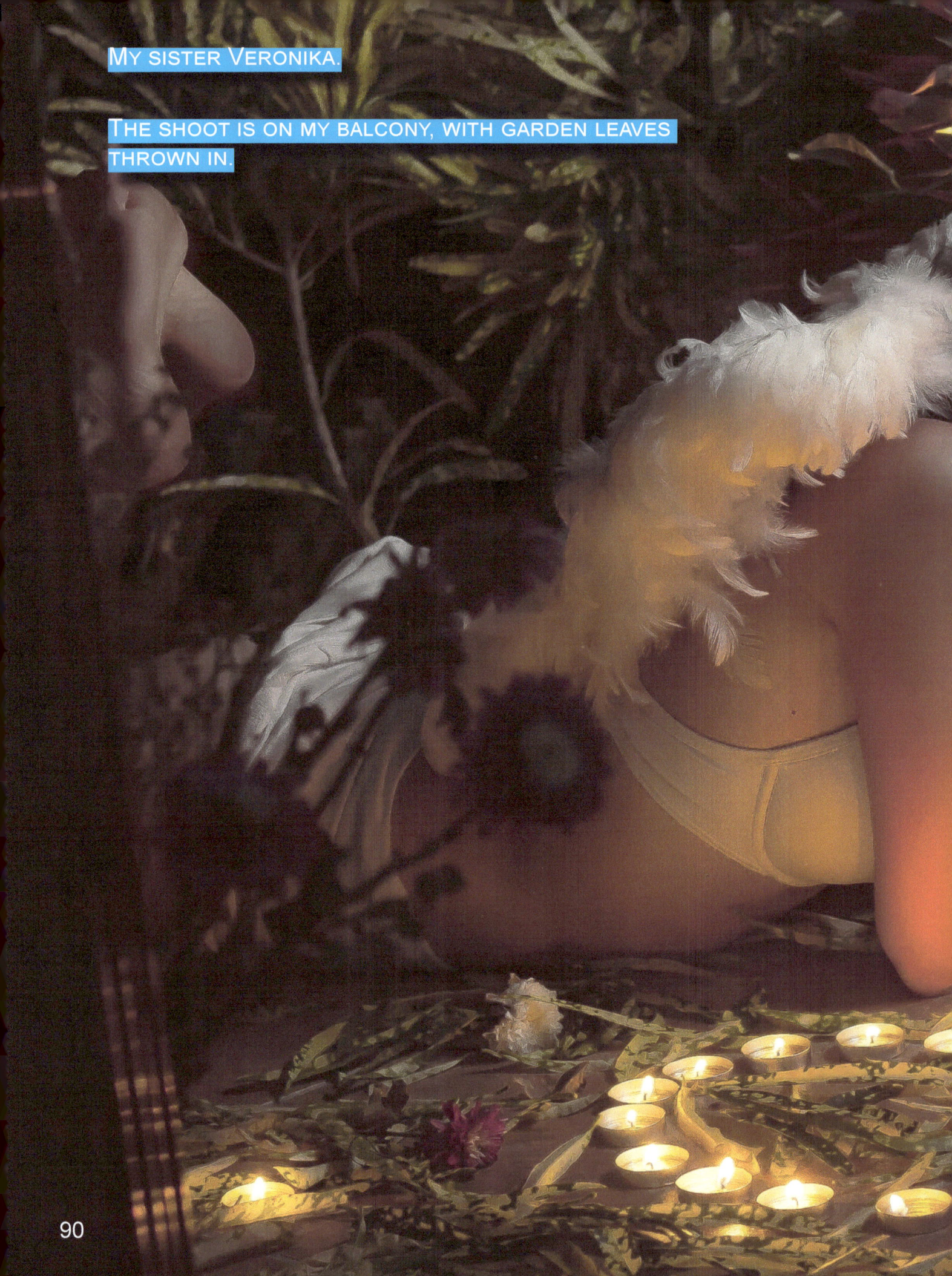

MY SISTER VERONIKA.

THE SHOOT IS ON MY BALCONY, WITH GARDEN LEAVES THROWN IN.

90

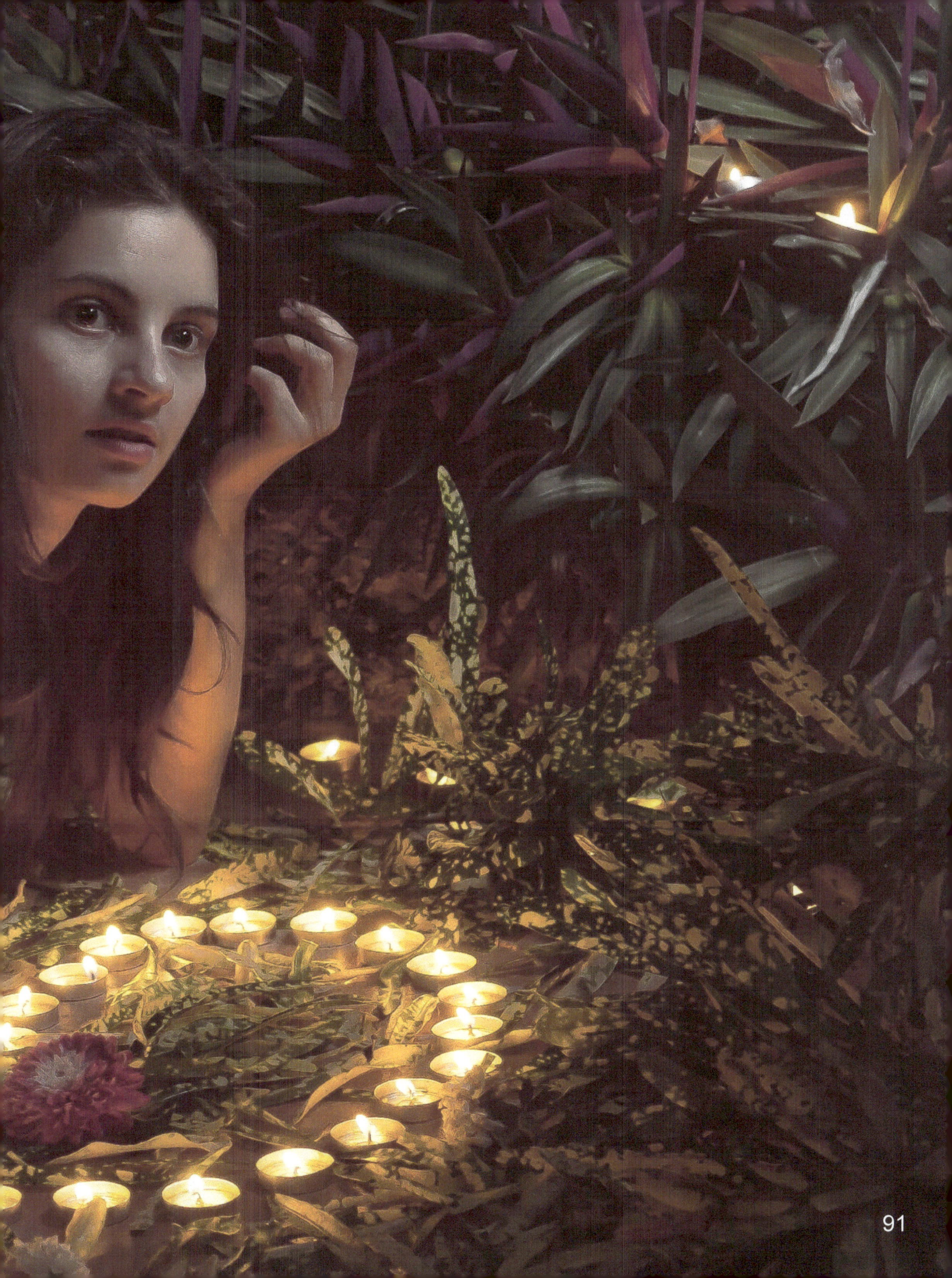

VERONIKA (SISTER) AT THE WHITE BEACH IN MOALBOAL

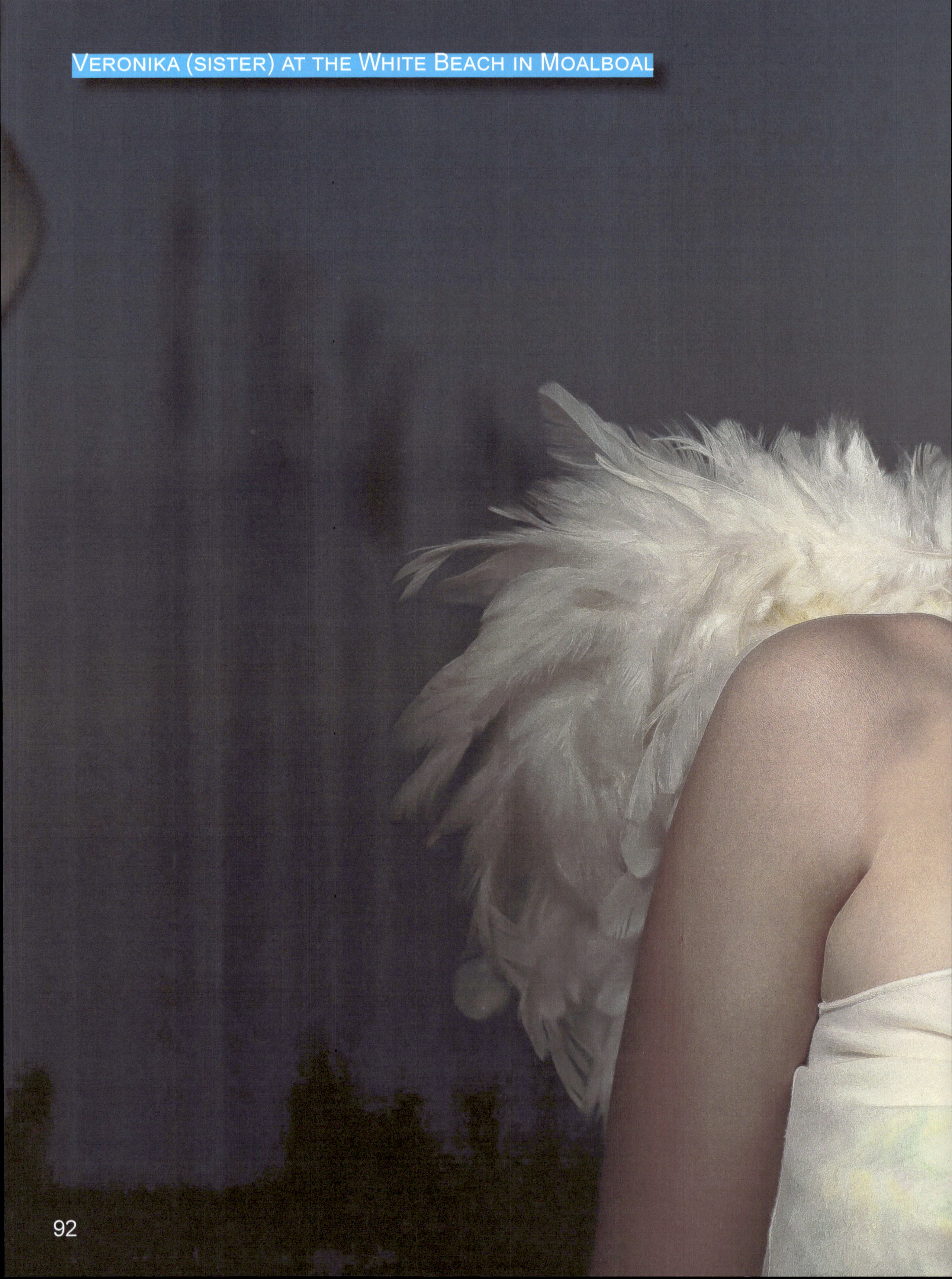

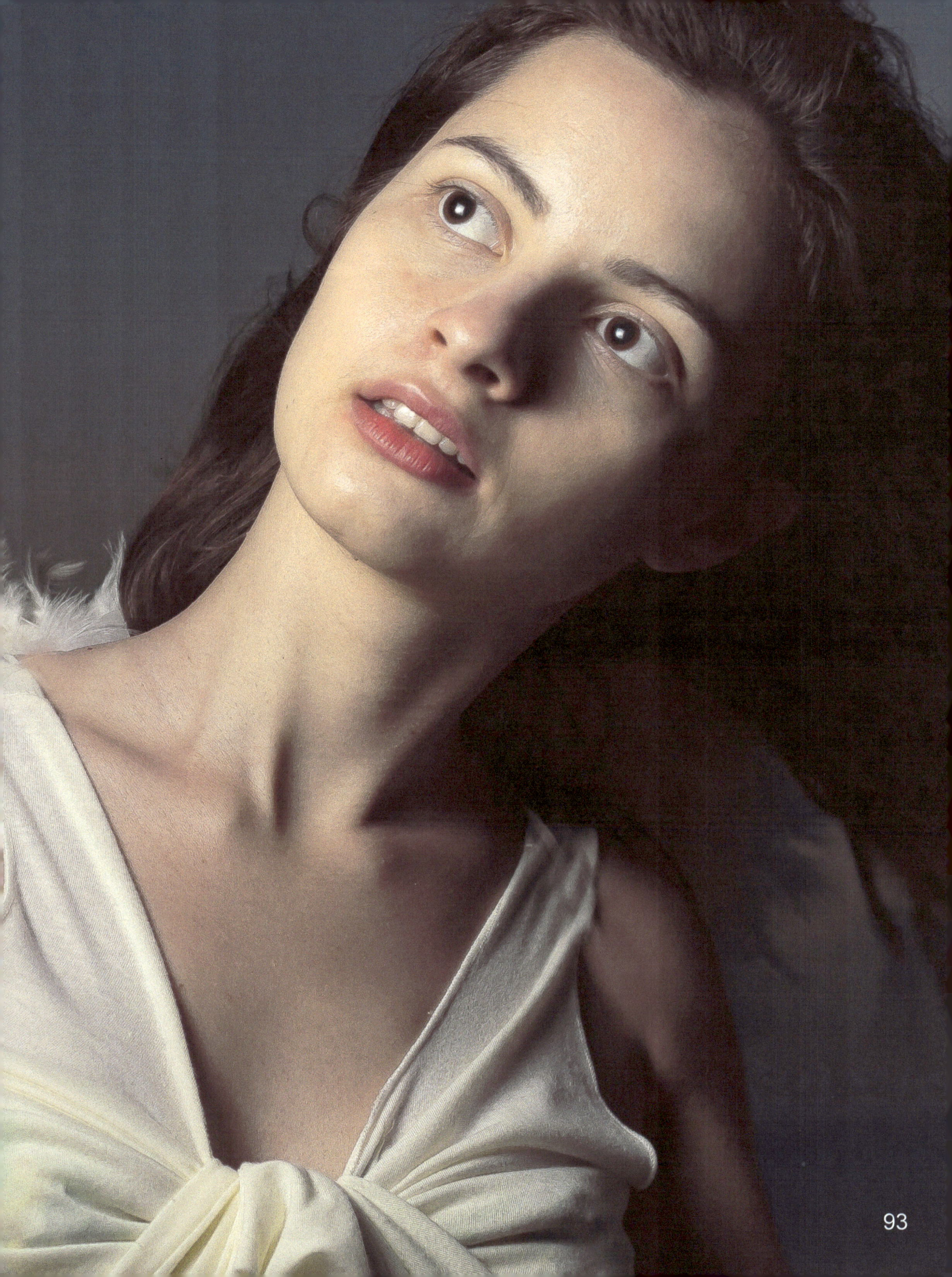

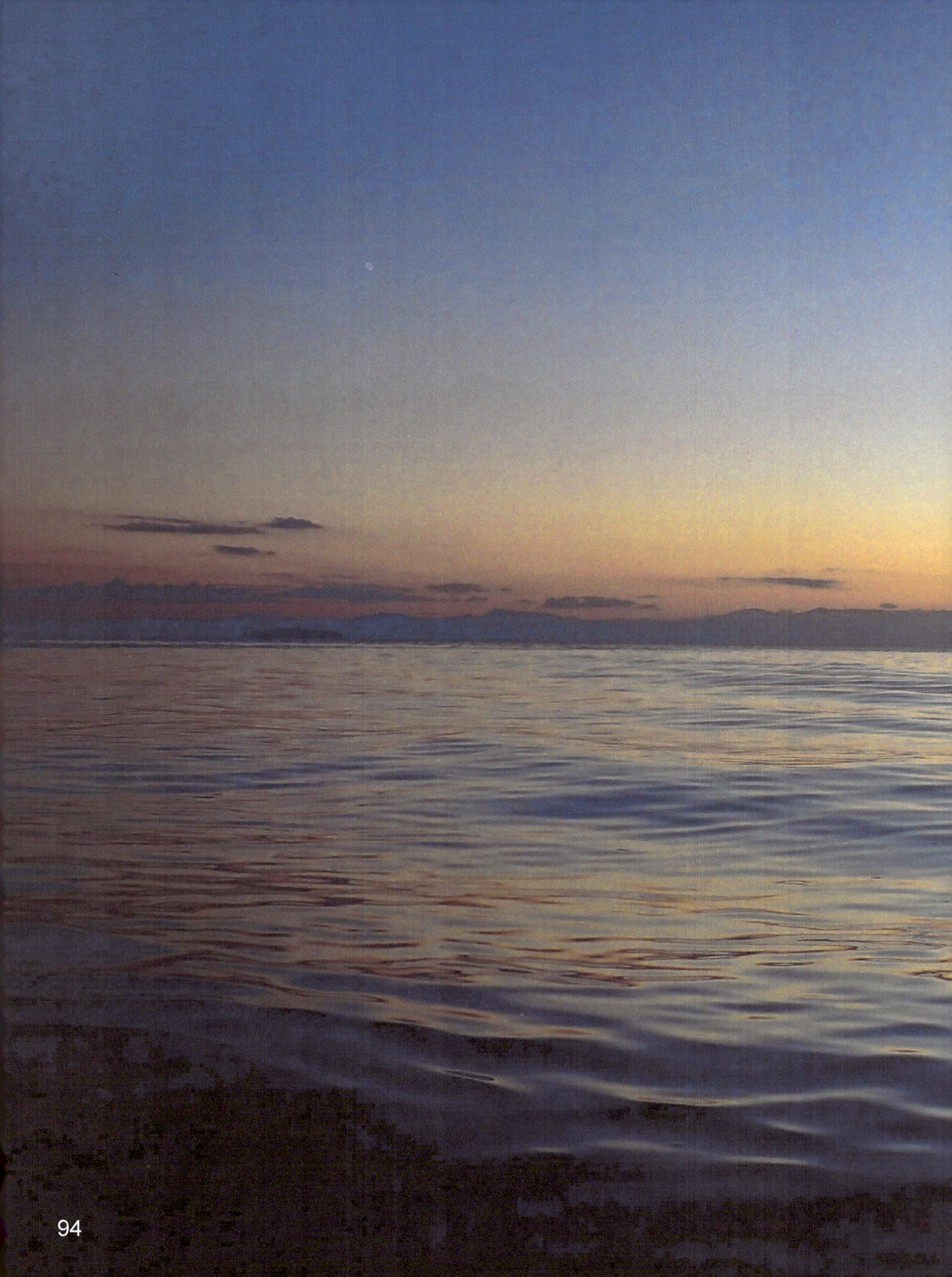

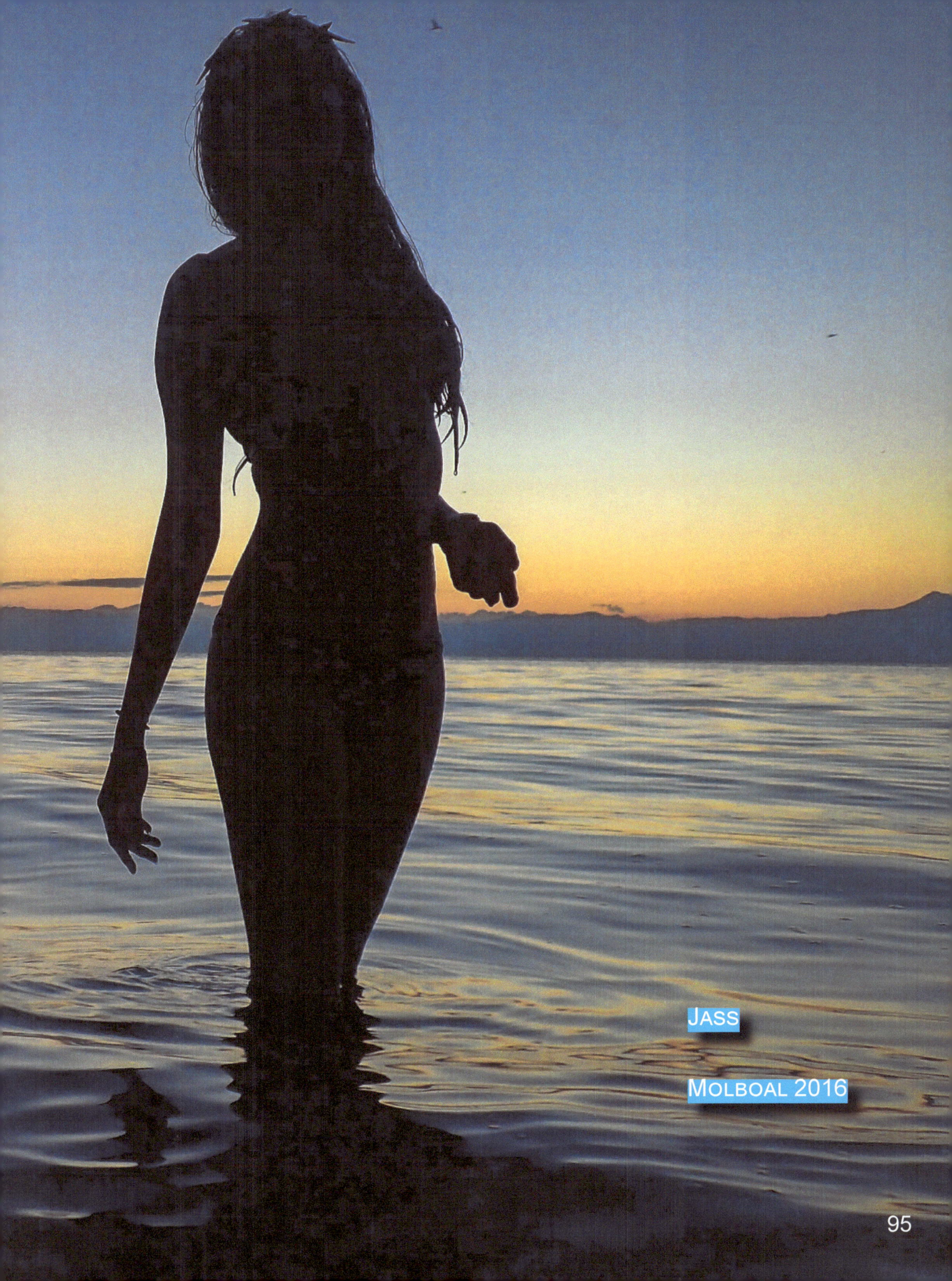

JASS

MOLBOAL 2016

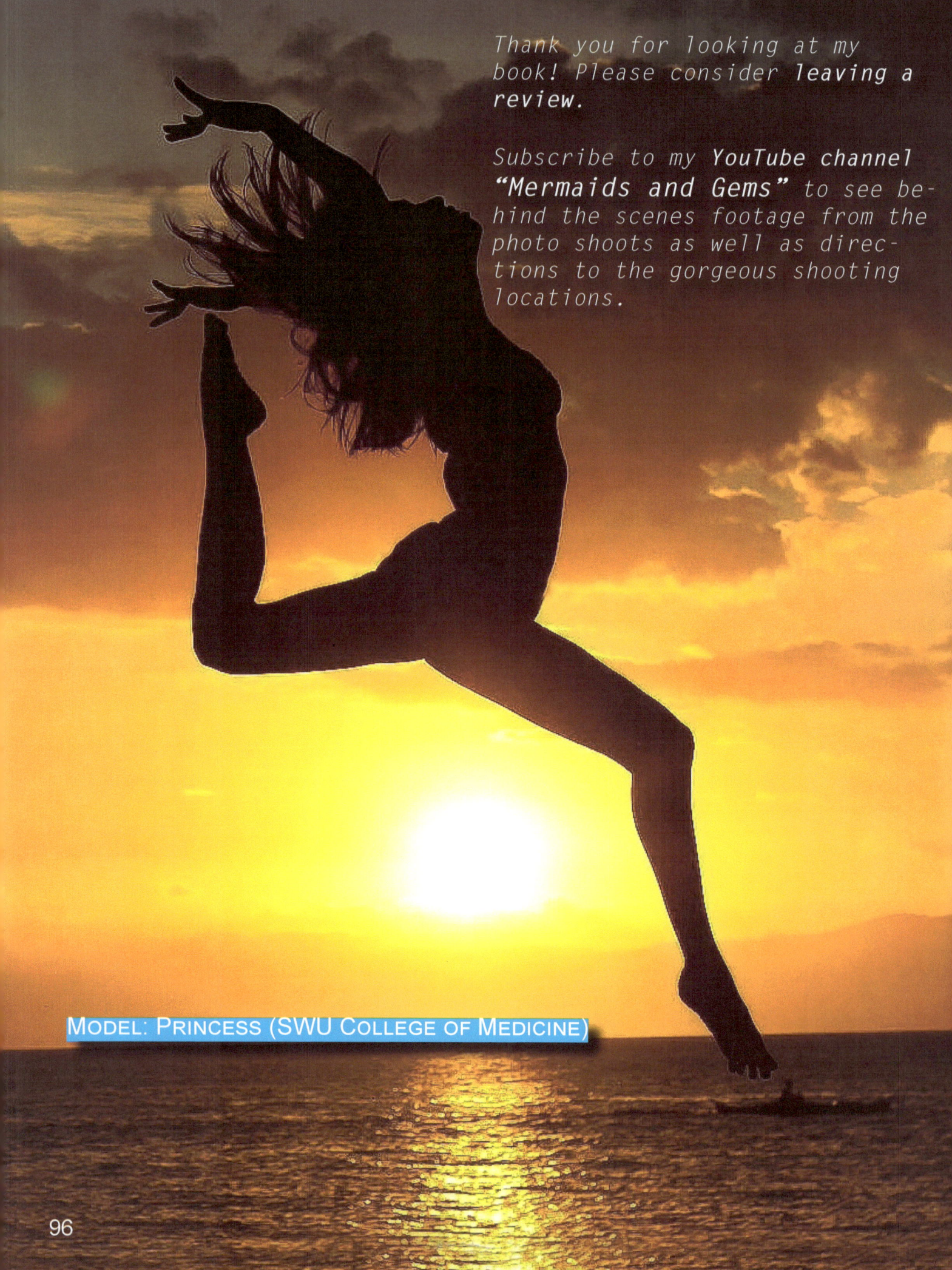

Thank you for looking at my book! Please consider *leaving a review.*

Subscribe to my *YouTube channel* **"Mermaids and Gems"** to see behind the scenes footage from the photo shoots as well as directions to the gorgeous shooting locations.

MODEL: PRINCESS (SWU COLLEGE OF MEDICINE)